Shirdi Sai Baba
The Divine Healer

Shirdi Sai Baba
The Divine Healer

Raj Chopra

STERLING PAPERBACKS
An imprint of
Sterling Publishers (P) Ltd.
A-59, Okhla Industrial Area, Phase-II,
New Delhi-110020.
Tel: 26387070, 26386209; Fax: 91-11-26383788
E-mail: mail@sterlingpublishers.com
www.sterlingpublishers.com

Shirdi Sai Baba: The Divine Healer
© 2012, Sterling Publishers Pvt. Ltd.
ISBN 978 81 207 9457 3
First Edition 2009
Revised and Enlarged Edition 2012

All rights are reserved.
No part of this publication may be reproduced, stored in a retrieval system or transmitted, in any form or by any means, mechanical, photocopying, recording or otherwise, without prior written permission of the original publisher.

Printed in India
Printed and Published by Sterling Publishers Pvt. Ltd.,
New Delhi-110 020.

Preface

Today there is no end to the books available on Shirdi Sai Baba. But this book, *Shirdi Sai Baba: The Divine Healer*, is different. Its uniqueness lies in its approach to the subject. It is a systematic, thematic presentation of facts in a simple and lucid manner. A cursory glance at the contents will confirm this view. The main aim has been to show Baba has been treating the ailing humanity in one way or the other.

What inspired me to write this book? I happened to get access to and read books by Sh. Narsimha Swami. Though, nobody can underestimate their value, I found them too voluminous for the average reader. They are full of sermons and Sanskrit slokas. Frankly speaking, not many of us know that much Sanskrit as to appreciate them. For me, at least, they did not serve any purpose. This is why I made it a point to exclude slokas from my book. Several other books on Sai Baba that I went through were no doubt full of information but lacked systematic presentation of facts. But I wanted to give my readers something easily comprehensible and compact. The book is now in your hands. I hope my efforts to simplify have succeeded and will be appreciated.

Acknowledgement

I would like to thank profusely, the Bhatnagar family who lent me books on Shirdi Sai Baba by Sh. Narsimha Swami, the foremost researcher of Baba. I am also thankful to Dr Rabinder Nath Kakarya who introduced me to Sh. S. K. Ghai, Director, Sterling Publishers. I am grateful to both as they have been instrumental in the publication of this book.

31st March, 2012 **Raj Chopra**

Contents

	Preface	v
1.	Pen Portrait of Sai Baba	1
2.	Baba's Disputed Identity	9
3.	Baba is God	15
4.	Baba is All Gods in One	18
5.	Omniscient Baba	30
6.	Image Worship	50
7.	Baba's Miracles	54
8.	Baba's Teachings	59
9.	Baba's Gravitational Pull	62
10.	Baba Saw Divinity in all Creatures	68
11.	Baba's Command Over Elements	74
12.	Male Child by Baba's Grace	77
13.	Baba as Protector/Saviour	82
14.	Baba as Helper	92
15.	Baba as Ashutosh	99
16.	Prayers Answered	101
17.	Udhi and Prayer to Cure	108
18.	Udhi, Prayer and Dream to Cure	110
19.	Udhi as Annapurna	112
20.	Baba's Appearance	113
21.	Baba as a Unique Doctor	117
22.	Baba's Appearance to Protect	151
23.	Baba's Appearance to Help	154

24.	Invisible Appearance	162
25.	Dream to Communicate	163
26.	Dream to Warn	174
27.	Dream to Cure	176
28.	Use of Voice	183
29.	Baba's Grace	186
30.	Baba and the Low-Caste	188
31.	Baba and Onion	190
32.	When Permission to Depart was not Granted	192
33.	Hindu–Muslim Unity	202
34.	Dakshina	206
	Bibliography	219
	Glossary	221

1

Pen Portrait of Sai Baba

In the words of Gangagir, "He (Baba) is a precious jewel. His worth is very high. It is the greatest luck of this village (Shirdi) that you have such a gem here."

Anandnath Maharaj, a disciple of Akalkot Maharaj says, "He is a diamond. You don't know his real worth. Though He may be on a dung hill, still remember that He is a real diamond." He said this at a time when Baba's value had not been realized and most of the people took him to be a mad faqir.

In *Sai Satcharita*, Hemadpant says, "When one gazes upon Baba's face, all hunger and thirst are gone. One forgets all miseries of earthly existence. Gazing into His eyes one loses sense of individuality. Bliss gushes out from within and the mind sinks into an expanse of sweetness." At another place he says that when Baba arrived at 'Chawadi', Sai's face shone with peculiar lustre. He beamed with a steady radiance and beauty and everyone admired Him to their heart's content.

On 12th January 1912, G.S. Kharparde wrote in his diary, "Baba gave me a yogic glance. I felt ecstatic the whole day." On 17th January, he wrote, "Baba smiled benignly. It is worthwhile spending years here (Shirdi) to see it even once. I was overjoyed and stood gazing like a madman."

When Baba went begging for alms, if someone looked into His eyes he/she used to get beatified and would desire any number of rebirths just to keep looking into Baba's eyes.

Mr Clerk, a Parsi, says whenever he went into Baba's presence he forgot everything. He had no trouble, no anxiety, no care, no fear. Everything was blotted out and he had a blissful time in Sai's company.

Ram Chander Vaman says that it always gave him (and other devotees) great relief to be in Baba's presence. Worries would leave one as soon as one came in His presence and happiness filled one's soul.

Mrs Manager says, "When I went and sat in His presence I always forgot my pain, and indeed, the body itself and all mundane cares and anxieties. Hours would pass by while I sat blissfully unaware of their passage. It was an extraordinary experience shared by all his true devotees." According to her, there was such power and penetration in Baba's glance that none could continue gazing into his eyes. One felt that he was reading him/her through and through. Soon one would lower his/her eyes."

Y.J. Galwanker says, "Once in 1917, I went to Shirdi. Baba put his hand over my head and, strangely, I forgot myself, my surroundings, everything, and went into a state of ecstasy."

In 1910, Harish Chander Pitale came to Shirdi from Mumbai. His son was a patient of epilepsy. Baba cast a glance at the child and within half an hour he was cured of the disease.

Balwant Hari Karnik visited Baba in 1911. He found such magnetism in Baba's eyes that he decided to visit Shirdi every year.

An orthodox Pathan, thinking that he should stop Baba once and for all from going astray by allowing the Hindus to worship him in the noisy way, rushed towards Baba with a big rod to murder Him. Baba simply cast a glance at him and caught his wrist. This slight gesture of Baba rendered him powerless and he fell to the ground and was able to get up only with the help of two persons.

Alchemic Personality

Baba had an alchemic personality, which could bring unbelievable transformation in others. He brought tremendous changes in the personality of Abdullah Jan. When he came to Shirdi, he regarded

Hindus as enemies. After staying there for three years his feelings of animosity vanished and he began to view them as his brethren.

Another man in whose life Baba brought unbelievable changes was Balabhat, a 'mamlatadar' of Kopergaon who was there for five years from 1904 to 1909. He used to say that Baba was a mad faqir and scoffed at those who visited Shirdi often. Once, some of his friends suggested that he should go and see Baba before forming his opinion of Him. So he accompanied them to Shirdi and stayed there for five days. On the fifth day Baba covered him with a *gerua*. From that day onwards he was a changed man. He would not leave Shirdi and join duty. So much so, Mr Dixit had to get his leave extended for one year. Even after a year he was mad after his guru. He was granted pension on compassionate grounds as he was suffering from religious melancholia. When his friends asked him the reason for his transformation he told them that the change came in him suddenly when Baba put the robe on him. 'Instantly,' he told them, "my earlier frame of mind was replaced with a new one, after which attending to worldly duties was unthinkable."

Despite his faults and foibles, Dass Ganu was one of the notable followers of Baba. His base metal of a petty-minded, lewd constable was turned into gold of a saint, who in turn moulded the spiritual destinies of tens of thousands of Sai devotees by his kirtans.

Baba was fully detached

C.K. Narke says Baba was a 'Brahmachari' and his glittering eyes shone with purity. He kept women at a distance. During the day a few women were allowed to massage his legs up to the knees. He was always clad and never indecently exposed.

Chakra Narain, a Christian, was not a believer. Even though he watched him sceptically, the result was to create in him a high regard for Baba. First and foremost was the fact that he was not moved by women and wealth. Many women came and bowed their heads at his feet or sat before him but he never cast even one glance of admiration or lust at them. He was clearly and unmistakably unattached.

Baba did not believe in hoarding

Mrs Manager says that one of the distinguishing features of Baba's life was freedom from care and anxiety. He had no personal interests to protect, no institution to seek support for, no private property to safeguard or feel anxious about. He lived on alms and voluntarily offered food. He did not seek any comforts. He even objected to the repair of the dilapidated 'Masjid'.

Arthur Osborne says, "He never possessed luxury, founded an 'ashram', erected buildings or acquired property, and when he died he had just enough money (Rs. 16) to pay for his funeral."

Baba received many donations but did not keep them for the next day. He distributed them then and there among the deserving.

Chakra Narain says that Baba was not moved by wealth or women. People voluntarily gave him money. Whatever he got, he distributed with a liberal hand. Often his receipts were smaller than his disbursements.

Kashinath Garde stayed at Shirdi for eight days, during which he witnessed a strange sight. Hari Sita Ram Dixit had returned after conducting some big case and with a trunk full of money, his fees—it may have been at least a thousand rupees in the form of silver coins. He placed the trunk before Baba as an offering. Baba dipped both his hands into the heap of coins and gave away fistfuls of these to the faqirs and others who were gathered there in crowds waiting for such windfalls. In a few minutes the all money was thus gifted away. Dixit was in no way disconcerted at the disappearance of his money.

Baba received a silver watch from Upasani Baba's brother and immediately gave it away to a person standing nearby.

Once a princess of a state brought a trunk full of gold for Baba. Baba asked Mhalsapathy to return it immediately.

Baba was impartial

Baba's 'darbar' was open to all. He was just and impartial. He was not obsequious to the rich and contemptuous of the lowly. He treated officials of high rank and the destitute or beggars with perfect equality.

Perin S. Barucha says dogs, cats, crows and lizards were as welcome as lepers were in Dwarkamai. The rich, the poor, the able-bodied and the handicapped, all were treated with the same graciousness and courtesy.

Once Cursetji Shahpuri Pestonji and his brother-in-law went to Shirdi. They were accommodated on the ground floor while rich people were accommodated upstairs. As they sat in the mosque, they thought, "What sort of justice is there in this darbar? Rich people are enjoying comforts above and poor people are left downstairs to suffer inconveniences." At this moment Sai Baba told someone present, "Take these people up," and they were given accommodation upstairs. This was, at once, proof of Baba's reading their minds and of his love for equality and justice.

Baba was against conversion

Among Baba's devotees were Christians, Muslims, Jains, Budhists, Parsis as well as Hindus, and He never expected anyone to convert from one religion to another. Once when a Hindu devotee who had embraced Islam was brought before Baba, Baba slapped him and exclaimed, "What! You have changed your father!"

Baba was against black magic

Once Khush Bhau, a magician, wanted to enter the Dwarkamai but was not allowed inside until and unless he gave up the use of black magic. He was fully compensated, though, by coming in contact with the alchemic personality of Baba. He was entrusted with that divine power to produce 'udhi' at will and cure people the way Baba used to do.

Baba was a lover of arts

Sometimes Baba used to tie bells around his ankles and sing and dance. His voice was so pleasant that whenever he sang with fervour not only the devotees, even animals used to be spellbound. They used to watch him dance and enjoy his music.

Baba was a polyglot

The fact is that even Dass Ganu did not know whether Baba knew how to read or write or even sign his name. But He was a polyglot. Urdu and Marathi were the languages that He used while interacting with the people. He also knew Sanskrit, a fact which nobody can deny because once He explained a particular Sanskrit stanza that even a learned Sanskrit scholar (Chandorkar) could not explain. This fact is confirmed by Chandorkar's children.

Shama, a primary schoolteacher then, slept in the school adjacent to the mosque. At night he could hear English, Hindi and many other languages being spoken in the mosque, evidently by Baba, who was its sole occupant.

Nana Sahib Chandorkar and his son Bapu Rao say that all the mantras that Baba uttered were either in Persian or in Arabic but not in Sanskrit.

As stated earlier, Baba had a great love for music and dance. In his early days he would often sing devotional songs, usually in Arabic or in Persian or Hindi songs of Kabir.

Duties first

Tired of his worldly duties, Haribhau Fanse left home for a pilgrimage to Rameshwaram. On the way he halted at Shirdi. When he went to seek permission to leave Shirdi for Rameshwaram, Baba asked him to go back home as his mother had begun fasting and if he did not go back she would die. Haribhau obeyed Baba and his mother was immensely pleased to see her son back.

Once a railway clerk got his leave sanctioned and passes made. However, as a railway strike was expected, his boss asked him to postpone the trip for the time being but the clerk was adamant. He would not listen to his boss. At night, Baba appeared in his dream and ordered him not to come to Shirdi. The clerk could not disobey Baba, so he got his leave cancelled. This pleased his senior as it became clear that he was not involved in the strike. A month later when he went to Shirdi, Baba said, "Don't be mad. You have as yet many responsibilities to discharge. So stay at home chanting my name." This clearly shows Baba's disapproval of his devotees' running down to holy places brushing aside their duties.

Baba was always mindful of His devotees' interests

Bapu Sahib Jog had lost his mother. As there was no learned Brahmin in Shirdi he wanted to go to Nasik to get the ceremonies performed but Baba would not permit him to leave Shirdi. On the last day, when the ceremonies were to be performed, a learned Brahmin reached Shirdi and did the desired work. So, there was no need for Bapu Sahib Jog to take the trouble to go to Nasik when Baba was there to bring a learned 'pandit' to Shirdi for him.

Baba took others' troubles on Himself

Hans Raj came to Shirdi with severe asthma, which troubled him day and night. Strangely, at Shirdi, it troubled him during the daytime only and abated at night. At the same time Baba was found coughing at night. Apparently, Baba had taken over his malady. (This has been stated by Hans Raj's widow, Kashi Bai.)

Mrs Kharparde's son was stricken with plague. She went to Sai Baba to seek permission to leave Shirdi so that her son could get proper medical aid in their hometown. Baba lifted his robe and there were four egg-sized buboos on his body. Baba had taken the killer disease on Himself. The patient got well without any medical aid.

To top it all, Sai gave up His life for Tatya, who was expected to die young, as foretold by astrologers. Death is not transferable but Baba got the latter's death transferred to Himself.

Baba was secular

Instead of merely preaching, teaching or forcing the ideals of secularism and communal harmony, He actually lived these ideas.

S. P. Rohela says, "Which Hindu saint would allow Muslims to read the Quran in their abode, and which Muslim saint would allow the Hindus to read their scriptures in their premises?" In fact, Sai Baba's teachings represent a garland of carefully chosen, sweetest flowers of morality and spirituality grown in the flowerbeds of different religions.

Baba's accessibility to all, at all hours was a remarkable feature and his Dwarkamai was a unique university, which taught secularism par excellence to all who visited it.

2

Baba's Disputed Identity

Was Baba a Hindu or a Muslim? There are people who believe He was a Muslim. They had their arguments to support it.

Baba was a Muslim

To the Muslims He was a 'pir', living in the Mosque, observing the discipline enjoined for a 'faqir', always uttering the Islamic 'Allah Malik'. His dress and the frequent use of Urdu confirmed that He was a Muslim.

Even Kharparde noted that all the mantras that Baba uttered were either in Arabic or in Persian, not in Sanskrit.

Baba came to Shirdi with a marriage party of Muslims. He wanted to enter the Khandoba temple but was not allowed to do so by Mhalsapathy because he thought Baba was a Muslim. He was persuaded to take shelter in a mosque because the Hindu natives of Shirdi felt that Sai Baba was a Muslim and so, unfit to take shelter in a Hindu temple.

Baba's worship in the mosque by the unsophisticated villagers stiffened the backs of the orthodox Hindus who abhorred the worship of a Muslim (which they thought Baba to be) by the Hindus in a mosque.

A Hindu railway employee of the Kopergaon railway station prevented people from going to Baba saying, "He is a dangerous and immoral man."

Nana Sahib Chandorkar's father had some unpleasantness with the local Muslims and so there came strict orders for all the family members not to have any connections with the Muslims. This came as a bombshell for Nana Sahib as he could not leave Baba whom he and everybody thought to be a Muslim.

Dass Ganu wanted to take a bath in the Sangam, where the Ganges and the Yamuna merge. Baba produced 'gangajal' from his toes. Dass Ganu sprinkled the holy water on his head but did not drink it lest it should pollute him, a Brahmin.

Minathai, Chandorkar's daughter, says that her father was so orthodox that he never drank the 'abhishek tirath' of Sai Baba.

Mr. and Mrs. Pradhan became Sai devotees. But their family pandit was unhappy that the Pradhans should worship a Muslim. Thus when their son Babu fell ill, he attributed it to the wrath of the Hindu gods.

A religious person of Satara wanted to teach Dass Ganu Vedantas, but the latter refused the offer because he relied on Baba for that. Then that person jeered at Baba and said that as a Muslim he knew nothing and could teach nothing of Vedantas.

A mamlatdar invited his doctor friend to accompany him to Shirdi. The doctor, a Ram 'bhakt', was unwilling to meet Baba who he thought was a Muslim. He was afraid that he might be obliged to bow to Him if he went there.

Moolay Shastri, an orthodox Brahmin well-versed in astrology, once came to Shirdi to see his friend Mr Booty, a millionaire of Nagpur, but stayed outside the mosque because Baba was a Muslim and he was a pure Brahmin.

One Marwadi from Navsari visited Baba with a few others but did not bow to Him as he seemed to be a Muslim faqir. Sai Baba glared at him and he, at once, left the mosque.

In 1894, Mhalsapathy was threatened by a Kazi with canes and lathies for worshipping Baba in the Hindu manner.

Twenty years later, a Pathan fanatic of the same orthodox, ignorant section came to Shirdi. He, too, hated the Hindus for spoiling Baba by worshipping him in the Hindu manner. It was night time when he came to Baba and told Him that he would kill them if only Baba permitted him to do that.

V.S. Eyer of Mayavaram arranged for 'Sai poojan' on 6th February 1944 and for that he requested M. Ganpathygal to perform the pooja. M. Ganpathyal however, declined the offer assuming Baba was a Muslim.

Another point that makes one feel that he was a Muslim is that he was a forceful advocate of the Muslim practice of circumcision.

Baba was a Hindu

To the Hindu devotees who saw divinity in Him, it was immaterial whether Baba was a Hindu or not. They flocked to him like flies attracted by sugar. To them Baba was and is a living god, inspiring, aiding and guiding them at every step of their life.

Baba told his close confidante Mhalsapathy, "I am a Brahmin of Pathari and when I was young, my parents gave me over to a faqir for being trained under him."

Shri B.V. Narsimha Swami, who spent twenty-nine years in Sai Baba's service, declares that Baba was born of Brahmin parents of Pathari, a village of the Nizam of Hyderabad and then given over to a faqir for being trained.

Prof. Narke has written that Baba once told him that his (Baba's) guru was a Brahmin. It is obvious that a Brahmin guru would not have accepted Baba as his disciple if the latter were Muslim.

When Dass Ganu visited Vasudevanand Saraswati in Andhra Pradesh, the great saint said to him, "Why did you come here instead of visiting Shirdi? My elder brother is there. People are under the impression that Sai Baba is a Muslim faqir but He is my elder brother."

When the family pandit of Mr. and Mrs. Pradhan attributed their son's illness to the wrath of Hindu gods, Baba appeared in his dream and told him that He was Dattatrey. But the pandit kept this a secret. When Babu's condition became serious, he ran to Baba's photo and prayed for the child's health and the child recovered immediately. Need we say that the pandit then realized that Baba was not a Muslim?

When Moolay Shastri came to meet his millionaire friend he remained outside the masjid because Baba was a Muslim. To his surprise, inside he found not Sai Baba but his guru Golup Swami sitting. In no time, he entered the masjid and prostrated before Baba.

M. Ganpathygal had turned down V.S. Eyer's request to perform the pooja at the Sai poojan. But on the chosen day at 5.30 a.m. he was directed by his guru to go and fulfil his duty and he obeyed.

According to S. Barucha, the Hindu followers regarded Him as an incarnation of various deities in their religion. In December 1912 when Swami Sharananand went to Shirdi, he was anxious about his father's life as he had dropsy and in those days it was considered to be a fatal disease. Unasked, Baba said to him, "Bring that big-bellied man here." Swami Sharananand said to himself, "How is it possible when he takes You to be a Muslim?" At this Baba said, "Am I not a Brahmin?" This shows that Baba considered Himself to be a Brahmin.

In 1916, Shantaram Balwant Nachane went to Shirdi. His friend V.S. Samant gave him a coconut and two annas to be offered to Baba. He offered the coconut but forget to offer the two annas. When he went to seek permission to leave Shirdi, Baba reminded him by saying, "You may go, but why have you been retaining the two annas of this poor Brahmin?"

Although on the behest of Mr Sathe, his master, Megha came to Shirdi to serve Baba, he was not happy because he believed Baba to be a Muslim. His hesitation offended Baba so much that He did not let Megha step into the Dwarkamai and was even prepared to hit him with a stone. This incident clearly shows Baba's dislike for those who shunned Him considering him to be a Musalman.

Baba's 'dhuni' that kept burning ceaselessly reminds one of a pure Brahmin, an 'agnihotri'. The 'tulsi brindaban' Baba had

Baba's Disputed Identity

constructed in the centre of the yard outside the mosque is another sign of his being a Hindu.

As noted by Kharparde, when Baba blew the conch it produced the sound 'aum'.

Meenathai says that Baba used the word 'Narain' so frequently that her father concluded He must have been a Brahmin 'sanyasi' as Brahmin sanyasis use this term very frequently.

Baba's Hindi was as fluent as his Urdu. Not only that, He knew Sanskrit so well that it pricked Chandorkar's pride, as he believed himself to be a learned scholar of Sanskrit.

Dattatrey Damodar Rasane says Sai had great respect for monkey-god Hanuman. There was a small image of Hanuman in the upper platform of the Chawadi. Once, Baba was sitting on the lower platform and it started raining. When water began to flow into the Chawadi, someone suggested to Baba to go to the upper platform. Baba refused to do so, saying, "How can I be seated on the same level as God?" Dattatrey further says that an orthodox Muslim brought a 'sehra' to be kept in the mosque but Baba directed him to put it on the image of Hanuman. Also, when 'aratis' of saints Jnandev and Tukaram, were sung, Baba would sit up and fold his palms in respect.

Gopal Rao Gund brought building material to get the mosque repaired but Baba used it to repair Shani 'Mandir' and Maruti Mandir instead.

After the birth of a son, Gopal Rao Gund wanted to honour Sai Baba by celebrating 'urs'. For this, Baba selected Ramnaumi day, a day sacred to the Hindus.

Baba named his abode, the masjid, Dwarkamai after Dwarka, the abode of Lord Krishna.

In the words of Abdul Baba, "I do not think any other Mohammedan except me read the Quran sitting by Baba's side, while there is no end to the list of Hindu scriptures which were read there."

Rajballi Mohd. Khoja says that he does not remember any prominent or scholarly Muslim who went to Sai Baba.

"When some Muslims offered prayers in the mosque, Baba never joined them," says E. Bhardwaj. He never allowed a 'tazia' to remain in the mosque for more than two or three days. After that He placed it on the dhuni saying, "I don't want a corpse in the mosque."

According to one biographer, a few hours before Baba breathed His last He told Tatya Patil that Brahmins alone should take care of His body. So the last rites of Baba were conducted by Bala Sahib Bhate and Upasani Baba.

Arthur Osborne says that Baba was a vegetarian like His Hindu followers.

3

Baba is God

Perin S. Barucha says Baba never used the expression "I am God', still innumerable cases have been recorded where thousands of His devotees have realized His omnipotence, omnipresence and omniscience. This is being experienced by several thousand more devotees today who concentrate on Him with love and devotion whether they are in Shirdi or miles away in their own abodes.

Baba had unaccountable and marvellous knowledge of things and events far removed from Him in the sense of time and space, and a remarkable power to foretell events or to force events to come to pass in accordance with His supreme will. Everyone noted with devout admiration that He would frequently mention either expressly or by allusions, their secret thoughts. He was also aware of their remote past, incidents of which they had lost all memory, or those which had occurred hundreds of miles away from His residence and which none could possibly have communicated to Baba.

This ability to read people's mind and foresee events was child's play for Baba. Other saints forget their body and surroundings and then return to it. They have to make an effort to trace the thoughts of others or read their past history. But Sai Baba was always in the all-knowing state.

Acharya E. Bhardwaj says Sai Baba's mission was to give blessings and He proved these in various ways—saving lives, protecting the vulnerable, averting accidents, granting offsprings, facilitating financial gain, bringing people into harmony with themselves and with each other, and affecting the transformation of those who came to Him. To his devotees He is nothing less than God.

Mhalsapathy was a fan of Kabir. Kabir, in his couplets, uses the word Sai for God. Mhalsapathy, taking Baba to be God, called Him Sai Baba.

Once Megha was sleeping in his room in the Sathe wada, with the door bolted from inside. A little later he saw Baba inside the room. Baba asked him to draw a trident on the shivlingam and sprinkled 'akshat' all over the place. When Megha woke up he found yellow rice strewn all over the place but Baba had disappeared. Later, when he met Baba, his first question to Baba was as to how He had entered through the bolted door. To this Baba replied, "Do you think Baba is only the physical body that you are seeing? I am everywhere. Walls and doors cannot obstruct my movement."

After the death of his wife, Balram Mankar went to Shirdi to stay with Baba. Baba sent him to Machhindergarh to meditate regularly. One day Baba gave him 'darshan' while he was in the conscious state. On being asked why he was sent to Machhindergarh, Baba replied, "While at Shirdi you imagined Me as a person made of five elements and three and a half cubits in length. You also thought that I am always in Shirdi. Now, say whether the Baba you see here and the Baba you saw at Shirdi are the same or not? I sent you here to prove this."

When the Rohilla who had come to kill Baba was humbled, he fell at Baba's feet and apologized. Baba raised His right hand in blessing and the Rohilla saw Mecca and Madina and the Quran Sharif in Baba's palm. He realized that He was not just a Muslim faqir but Allah Himself.

C.G. Narke says Sai Baba is God, not just 'satpurush'. He says, "When Baba talked He spoke as one seated in my heart, knowing all my thoughts, all my wishes etc. This is God within. I have no hesitation in saying He is God. I tested him at times. Each incident strengthened my belief that He is all-knowing, all-seeing and able to mould all things to His will."

Rao Bahadur S.B. Dhumal says that Baba could and did foresee things far ahead and took every required step to avert the evil and accelerate the good that was coming to him.

In 1932, M.G. Pradhan's son had very high fever. On the third or fourth day his pulse seemed to be missing. The doctor who was brought in to check the boy declared him dead. Pradhan was grief stricken but unwilling to accept the doctor's view. He took some 'udhi' of Baba, applied it on the child's forehead and placed one of Baba's photos at his bedside. The doctor told Mr Pradhan that he was being superstitious. But the latter was convinced that Baba was God and would save the boy. After about forty-five minutes the boy regained consciousness and actually got up and began to play!

4

Baba is All Gods in One

Sai Baba exemplified the Hindu belief that all gods are manifestations of one Supreme Power. He appeared to His devotees in the form of the deity they worshipped. In the words of Perin S Barucha, "Many a man who had gone to Shirdi with friends or relatives out of simple curiosity, privately determined not to bow before the controversial faqir of uncertain origin, was astonished to find himself in the presence of his beloved deity in place of the white-robed figure he had expected to find."

Baba as Dattatrey

In about 1900, one Bala Sahib Binnewala, a close relative of Nana Sahib Chandorkar, went to Sai Baba, only to oblige Nana Sahib. He was a worshipper of Lord Dattatrey. When he went and saw Sai Baba, the latter appeared to him as having the three heads of Lord Datta. Bala Sahib was at once convinced that Sai Baba is/was Datta.

In 1911, Sonkar Balwant Khojokar's father went to Shirdi to attend Dattatrey Jayanti celebrations. Baba, sitting in the Dwarkamai, was surrounded by devotees. All of a sudden He started saying, "I am having labour pangs. I cannot bear it. I am about to deliver." Evidently He was identifying Himself with Anusuya, the mother of Dattatrey. Shortly after that He sent every one from the Mosque. After a while He called them in. His father was also among them. At Baba's seat he saw a three-faced figure of a child. This happened for a moment and then he saw Baba in His usual form. This made him realize that Baba is Dattatrey.

Once, two visitors came to Shirdi form Goa. Baba asked one of them for fifteen rupees as 'dakshina' and refused to accept 'dakshina' when the other visitor offered thirty-five rupees of his own sweet will. Why? Because the first visitor when he was jobless had vowed to offer his first salary to Dattatrey. His first salary was fifteen rupees per month. This job had been Baba's boon to him. But he had forgotten to fulfill his promise. The force of 'karma' took him to Shirdi. By revealing His knowledge of the vow and the circumstances in which it was made and also by demanding the dakshina, Baba showed that He was Dattatrey.

Shinde had seven daughters and no son. He prayed to Dattatrey for a son and he got a son within a year but for six years he did not go to Gangasagar to thank his deity. (Gangasagar is only 200 miles from Shirdi.) When he visited Baba at Shirdi He flared up and said to him, "Are you so conceited and so stiff-necked? Where was any male progeny in your fate? I tore up this body (pointing to His own body) and gave you a male child in answer to your prayer and you don't have the courtesy to fulfill your vow even."

Dattatrey is shown surrounded by animals, mainly dogs. It may be recalled that dogs were favourites of Shirdi Sai Baba. At Shirdi even now it is considered to be an act of piety on the part of the devotees to offer milk to the dogs near the Dwarkamai.

Baba as Vithal

Nana Saheb Chandorkar was transferred to Pandharpur, the seat of the God he worshipped. Since he was to take charge immediately, he forthwith left for Pandharpur and on the way he felt he might as well go to Shirdi and get Baba's blessings and 'udhi'. When he had reached Neemgaon, Baba who was sitting with Mhalsapati and others in the Mosque at Shirdi said, "Let's do some bhajan today. Let's sing together." In no time the people went and brought musical instruments and began to sing a 'bhajan' which was led by Baba Himself. The refrain of the song was, "I have to go now and stay at Pandharpur, the place of my Lord and see Vithal there." When Nana Saheb came and heard this song sung by Baba, he was fully convinced that Baba was the living form of Vithal.

Balaram Dhurandhar of Bombay was an advocate. He was a devotee of Pandharpur Vithal. Once his brothers Babaji and Vaman Rao happened to see Baba. They were all praise for Him. Balaram heard about Baba's miracles from his brothers. A desire to go and see Baba was born in him. So in 1912, the Dhurandhar brothers left for Shirdi. It was Thursday. They were lucky to see the Chavadi procession. During 'arati' time Balaram Dhurandhar saw the lustre of Pandurang on Baba's face. The next morning too, when 'kakad arati' was being done to Baba, he saw the lustre of his beloved deity on His face.

The Raghubir Purandher's mother was pressing her son to go to Pandharpur and have the 'darshan' of Vithal but Purandhar never cared to and mentioned this to Baba. But Baba Himself one day broached the subject and asked that lady when she hoped to leave for Vithal's 'darshan'. Then He Himself gave his mother and his wife 'darshan' of Pandurang and Rukmani in the Mosque itself. Both the ladies were highly pleased and thereafter did not wish to go to Pandharpur and later whenever Baba asked the mother when she proposed to go to Pandharpur, the lady always replied that Sai Baba was her Vithal and Shirdi her Pandharpur. So she need not go away from the living God.

There was one Gauli Bua. He was a very pious old man. He used to go to Pandharpur very frequently to have 'darshan' of Vithal. As Shirdi is on the way. He used to go there also. He used to say he saw his Vithal in Baba.

Bhagwantrao's father worshipped Vithal regularly with great devotion. After his death his son neglected the worship and the annual pilgrimage to Pandharpur. When Bhagwantrao came to Shirdi, Sai Baba said to the other devotees pointing at him, "His father was my friend. So I drew him here. This fellow never offered 'navaidya' (offerings of food to the gods) and he starved Me and Vithal. I have drawn him to this place so that I could remonstrate with him and set him to carry on worshipping regularly." Bhagwantrao marvelled at Baba's words and his devotion was revived.

Baba as Krishna

It was 13th December 1980. Mrs. Sitaram Murti felt there were no instances of Baba having appeared to devotees in the form of Krishna, her favourite deity. The same evening she noticed the black and white framed picture of Baba had mysteriously turned sky blue in colour. When remarked on by some one that it was an indication that Baba was displeased with her, she panicked. The same night Baba appeared in her dream and said that she was needlessly panicking by the signs and that if she put three flowers on the picture the next day He would depart. She did as was directed. By the next evening the picture returned to its normal colour. In this way Baba demonstrated to the lady that Lord Krishna and He are no different.

This happened in Baba's childhood. One day Babu (as Baba was known as a boy) was playing with the son of a neighboring money lender. The boy lost all his marbles to Babu. Then he went to his mother's 'pooja room' and seizing the 'saligram' (a black stone meant for pooja), played with it. This also he lost to Babu. He expected Babu to return it but Babu put the 'saligram' in his mouth. So, the boy went to his mother and told her that Babu had taken her 'saligram' through foul play. Horrified, she rushed to the 'pooja room' and found the 'saligram' missing. She ran towards Babu and requested Him to return it. But Babu sat tight-lipped and refused to open his mouth. She then compelled him to open his mouth and saw in it what Yashoda had seen in Krishna's mouth. The whole cosmos was before her eyes. She realized that He was divine. She prostrated before Him then and there. Thereafter she went to Babu's house every day to touch His pious feet. Perhaps she was the first person to see divinity in Baba.

There is another episode which reminds one of Krishna who welcomed Sudama and ate the parched rice offered by him with great relish. It was Ram Naumi day. There were huge crowds at the Dwarkamai. Even the police was there to keep the surging crowds under control. At 11 am Baba's devotees wanted the police to stop the people from visiting the Dwarkamai as it was Baba's breakfast time but Baba said that He did not want to have breakfast. There was an old woman in the crowd who was finding it difficult to have Baba's 'darshan'. At Baba's request Tarkhand helped her to reach Baba. When she came Baba blessed her and said, "I have been waiting for you. Tell Me what have brought for Me to eat?" She had brought one loaf of bread and two onions. On the way, she had eaten up half the loaf and one onion. She gave the other half of the loaf and one onion to Baba. Baba ate it up and remarked, "How sweet they are!" This episode reminds one of Krishna's love for Sudama.

Another episode also leads one to Krishna. One evening a terrible storm threatened Shirdi. Thunder and lightning were followed by a torrential downpour. The village was flooded and anticipating disaster, people rushed to the Dwarkamai for help. Standing at the gate of the Mosque Sai Baba looked up at the sky and shouted at the elements to stop their fury and within minutes the rain subsided and all was calm. One is reminded of Krishna who lifted the Govardhan Parbat on his little finger to save the people who had come for help.

Both had similar fate in one more respect. They never had the good fortune to be nurtured by their biological mothers. It was the adoptive mothers who had the good luck to bring them up.

Bootywada was ready. Booty Saheb wanted Baba's permission to get the idol of Murlidhar (Krishna) made. In response to his question Baba asked him if He was not Murlidhar Himself. Iintially Krishna's statue was to be installed where now we have the statue of Baba.

B. Kishna's father once vowed to offer coconuts to Shiva but forgot about it. Baba appeared in B. Krishna's dream and demanded coconuts which were promised by his father.

Baba as Rama

A Brahmin doctor who worshipped Shree Ram as his God once went to Shirdi with a Mamlatdar as his guide on the express condition that he should not be forced to pay obeisance to Baba whom he considered to be a Muslim faqir. After reaching the Mosque, his friend went inside but the doctor stood outside for a couple of minutes and casually looked in to see what was going on. Suddenly, the doctor rushed in and fell at Baba's feet. Naturally, the Mamlatdar was surprised and later asked him why he had given up his earlier resolve. He said he saw his Ram where Baba was standing. So he could not control himself. He said Baba is not a Muslim faqir but an incarnation of Rama. Even three days later Baba graced him with the experience of supreme bliss which lasted for a fortnight.

In 1916, a Madrasi Bhajan party consisting of a man, his wife, his sister-in-law and his daughter, started on a pilgrimage to Banaras. On the way they heard of Baba's greatness and His generiosity in rewarding devotional singers and so they visited Shirdi. They sang several songs melodiously at the Dwarkamai but except for the man's wife who was very devoted to her chosen deity Ram all of them were singing with their hearts set on Baba's gifts of money. At the noon 'arati' Baba was so pleased with the woman's devotion that He graced her with the 'darshan' of Rama in His own person. The result was she was lost in spiritual bliss. Her eyes overflowed with tears of joy as she clapped her hands in utter joy. While every one saw Sai Baba in the Mosque she saw Ram in His place. She saw this vision not once but several times as long as she was in Shirdi. She was convinced that Baba is not a mere saint but Ram Himself. Her husband, however, did not believe her story and thought his wife was simply imagining things. One day, Baba had to appear in his dream just to convince him that his wife was not making up cock and bull stories.

Baba as Ganesha

Smt. Savitri Tendulkar, a housewife, was a victim of severe headaches. When all medical aid failed she turned to Baba. As soon as she bowed to Him, her ailment vanished quite mysteriously. She told this to Baba. Baba said that it was in return for all the fruits she had been feeding Him and the flowers she had been offering Him, all through her life. The lady was surprised as it was her first visit to Shirdi and she was seeing Baba for the first time. How could she feed Him sumptuously? At this Baba asked her whom she had worshipped since childhood. "Ganesha", said she. Baba said that all the fruits and flowers she had offered to Ganesha, had come to Him.

Chidamber Keshav Gadgil, probably the first devotee of Baba from outside Shirdi, was a worshipper of Ganpati and whenever he came to Shirdi and did his 'pooja' to Baba he believed that he was worshipping Ganpati. Once when Gadgil was offering 'pooja' to Baba, Baba told the people, "This cunning man always spies a rat under Me."

Baba as Satyanarain

In 1931 Sh. M V Sahastrabudh had a vision. He saw Satyanarain pooja going on in the Abhishake hall of the Samadhi Mandir. The offerings made to the image were passing straight to the tomb of Sai Baba. On enquiry, Sahastrabudh came to know that Satyanarain pooja was performed at that time at that place. This shows that Sai Baba is Satyanarain and Satyanarain is Baba.

Baba is Vishnu

In his infancy, Rege's family deity was Durga. At the age of eight, he was led from Durga to Vishnu. He was so attached to Vishnu that he wanted to attain the status of Dhruva. His concentration and prayers bore fruit in 1910, when he was 21 years old. He had three dreams in quick succession. In the first dream he left his body, on the bed and kept watching over it as if he were separate from it. Then he found that he was standing face to face with Vishnu. An hour later he had another dream. But this time, there was another figure standing next to Vishnu. Vishnu pointing to that figure told him, "This Sai Baba of Shirdi is your 'guru'. You must seek Him." Here the dream ended. After an hour or so, he had another dream. Now, he found that he was flying. By and by, he came to a village and enquired its name. When told that it was Shirdi, he wanted to know if Sai Baba lived there. Ultimately he was guided to the Mosque where Sai Baba was sitting with his legs out-stretched. He placed his head at Baba's feet and Baba placed His head at Rege's feet. That was the end of the third dream. It left an indelible impression on his mind. He wanted to go to Shirdi in search of his 'guru' but he could not as he was yet a student, dependent on others. After some time he did succeed in going to Shirdi and found his 'guru.' But was Baba just a 'guru' to him? Let us see what he has to say. "I look upon Baba as the Creator, Preserver and Destroyer. I did so before His 'samadhi' in 1918 and I do so even now," said he when he was interviewed by Sh. Narsimha Swami almost two decades after Baba's 'samadhi'.

Baba as Narsimha

Sadashiv Joshi of Sholapur accompanied his friend Gadgil to Shirdi. There he used to attend the daily 'arati' to Baba's photo in the Sathewada. On three days in succession Sadashiv had 'darshan' of Lord Narsimha in Sai's picture.

Baba as Khandoba

Once Martand, Mhalsapati's son, was sitting on the steps of the Khandoba temple. Baba walked towards Khandoba's idol and merged in it. Martand peeped behind the idol but there was no one. While he looked on in panic, Baba walked out of the idol and left the temple smiling at him. This incident made him feel that Baba is Khandoba and Khandoba is Baba. From then on Martand took to worshipping the idol as Baba's own form and this he did to the end of his life.

Some backward class people complained to Baba that they were not allowed to enter the Khandoba temple to have 'darshan' of the God. Baba told them that even He Himself was not allowed to enter the temple earlier because Mhalsapati thought that He was a Muslim faqir. Now the same Mhalsapati does not take even a drop of water without worshipping Him. He assured them 'darshan' of the deity. In no time the temple was transferred to the Dwarkamai. Everyone had full darshan of God. When they lifted their heads they found that they were at the feet of Sai Baba. They then realized that Sai Baba is Khandoba, Khandoba is Sai Baba.

Baba as Christ

Once, a priest named Thomas came to Shirdi to see Baba. It was Thursday. He could not enter the Dwarkamai, as it was overcrowded. He tried again and again but every time he was asked to wait. It was an insult to the ruling British, that a member of the government should be asked to wait and not be given a warm welcome. He sent a message to Baba that he was going back. Baba asked him to leave the next day but he would not listen. So he left and on the way he met with an accident and was hospitalized at Kopergaon. At midnight, Baba appeared to him and blessed him. He told him that He knew about the accident that was going to happen. He could have even been killed. But He saved him from the clutches of death. Then, the priest realized that there is no difference between Christ and Sai Baba.

Baba as Maruti

Nana Sahib Nimonkar served Baba from the beginning. Once, he had to go out of station for four days. He asked his son Somnath Deshmukh to take charge of Baba's pooja during his absence. During that short period he had a blessed vision. Baba was sitting in His usual place. Shyama was sitting beside Him. And suddenly the usual figure of Baba vanished and in His place Somnath saw the beautiful body of Hanuman. Only he could not see if a tail was attached to that body. Seeing that form he, at once, turned to Shyama and said, "Take His 'darshan'. He is Hanuman, Maruti". But before Shyama could turn his head, the vision had disappeared.

Baba as Akkalkot Maharaj

Harishchand Pitale of Bombay went to Shirdi with his son who had frequent fits of epilepsy and in a miraculous way, his son was cured by Baba. After staying there for several days when he went to seek permission to leave Shirdi Baba said, "Bhau, I have already given you two rupees. Now take these three notes and worship them. Allah will bless you." Pitale accepted those rupees but wondered what Baba meant when He said He had given him two rupees earlier, as that happened to be his first visit to Shirdi. Pitale then returned to Bombay with those three rupees and told his mother what Baba had said and asked her if she could make any meaning out of those cryptic words. His mother, too, was baffled at first but after some thinking she remembered an old incident in her life and was able to solve the mystery. "Just as you had now gone to Shirdi with your son," said the lady, " your father too had gone to Akkalkot when you were a child. Maharaj gave two rupees to your father to be kept in the shrine and worshipped and accordingly he worshipped those coins till his death but after his death that worship was not done and with the passage of time the coins were also lost. After some years even the memory of those coins was gone. Now Akkalkot Maharaj in Baba's form, has reminded you of your forgotten duty."

In 1904, when a devotee was preparing to go to Akkalkot. Akkalkot Maharaj appeared in his dream and told him that there was no need to come to Akkalkot as he was there at Shirdi in the 'avtar' of Sai Baba. When the devotee visited Sai Baba, the latter said that Akkalkot Maharaj and He are no different.

Bapusahib Jog, who was earlier devoted to Swami Samarth of Akkalkot, similarly served Sai Baba. One day, he demanded that Sai Baba should grant him the 'darshan' of Swami Samarth. During 'arati' Baba appeared to him in the form of the saint of Akkalkot.

Baba as Guru Golup Swami

Once Mooley Shastri, an orthodox Brahmin from Nasik, well-versed in the Shastras, went to Shirdi to meet his millionaire friend Bapusahib Booty of Nagpur. In the morning both of them went to the Dwarkamai. Since he was a plamist he wanted to study the supernatural Faqir's palm but Baba ignored his request. Mooley Shastri went back to take a bath. In the meanwhile, Baba asked

Booty to get Him 'dakshina' from his Brahmin friend Mooley Shastri. Mooley Shastri was puzzled when Booty conveyed Baba's message. He was a pious Brahmin used to receiving 'dakshina' from others. He wondered why he should offer 'dakshina' to a Muslim but he could not refuse because his millionaire friend was asking for it and moreover he (Booty Sahib) was very much devoted to Baba. So, very reluctantly he left his pooja unfinished and accompanied him to the Mosque and stood some distance away from the Mosque lest he be defiled as he had bathed. But from there he threw flowers at Baba and folded his hands in salutation. And lo! It was not Sai Baba who was seated in the Maszid. He saw his late Guru, Golup Swami there. He darted into the Mosque and fell at the feet of his Guru. While the congregation was chanting the "arati of Sai Baba, he was ecstatically calling out the name of his Guru standing there with folded hands his eyes closed in bliss. When he opened his eyes he saw not his Guru but Sai Baba asking him for 'dakshina'! Seeing Baba's real nature, Mooley Shastri completely forgot his pride of caste and learning. With tears of joy in his eyes, he gladly offered his 'dakshina'.

Baba as Moula Sahib

Rustamji Wadia of Nanded was a wealthy Parsi gentleman. He was unhappy because he did not have a child to enjoy his wealth. He opened up his heart before Das Ganu who recommended him to go to Shirdi to seek Baba's blessings. He got ready to go there without wasting his time. But before he left for Shirdi he invited a local maulvi and Das Ganu for tea to his house. He served them both with dainty dishes. In Shirdi Baba asked him for a 'dakshina' of five rupees and at the same time He added that He had already received three rupees and fourteen annas. (In those days a rupee had sixteen annas). Rustamji could not understand what Baba said but he paid the balance of one rupee and two annas. It was his first visit to Shirdi. When did he pay to Baba three rupees and fourteen annas? The question puzzled him. Next when he met Das Ganu, he told him what was puzzling him. Das Ganu asked him to check his accounts of the day when he entertained the Maulvi Sahib. When the accounts were checked it was found that he had spent exactly that amount on entertaining him. In this way, Baba made him realize that the Maulvi and Baba were no different.

Choker Ajgonkar raises the question: "Who was Baba? Ram ,Krishan or Shiva?" In fact, Baba manifested all forms of Godhood through His mortal frame before His worthy devotees.

To conclude, we can say that God incarnates in a new form in every age for the establishment of a 'dharma', for the destruction of the wicked and for the protection of the righteous.

5

Omniscient Baba

*B*aba dwelt in all things. Time and distance had no meaning for Him. He could know anything and everything that was happening within you. Neither the past nor the future, was hidden from Him. Baba once said to His devotees, "Whatever you do, wherever you may be, ever bear in mind that I am always aware of everything." What a great source of confidence to His devotees and yet what an effective check on their evil propensities!

Once, his daughter's parents-in-law insisted that Mhalsapati should dine with them. The omniscient Baba warned Mhalsapati. "You are going to be insulted." And he was insulted, as they had dined before he reached their place. On another occasion, he beat a sick bitch in a nearby village. When he came to the Dwarkamai Baba got angry with him and said that in a neighbouring village there was a sick bitch and people were giving her a lot of trouble. At this Mhalsapati got the hint that Baba was referring to him and apologized.

It was the occasion of an eclipse. Chandorkar had gone to Kopergaon to have a dip in the holy waters of the Godavari. Baba, sitting in the Dwarkamai, showed a four anna piece to the people sitting there and said that He had received that from Nana. When Nana Sahib came to Shirdi, people were curious to know how much he spent on charity. He admitted that he had given four annas in charity.

A student of yoga who had studied a lot about yoga but had no practical experience, once went to Shirdi accompanied by

Nana Sahib Chandorkar hoping that with Baba's blessings, all his problems could be solved. But when he went to the Mosque, he saw Baba eating stale bread with onions and for a moment he wondered how such a man, eating stale bread with onions, could solve all his problems and render him help in getting peace of mind that he needed. Baba who had read the visitor's mind said, "Nana, he that has the power to digest should eat onions and nobody else." When that yogabhyasi heard these words from Baba he was struck by Baba's omniscience and ran to Him and prostrated at His feet.

Prof. Narke, a talented scientist and the son-in-law of Mr. Booty, was unemployed for some time. He was so desperate that he felt a faqir's life suited him. Once in 1914 Baba was distributing 'kafanis' (long gowns meant for faqirs) to a number of devotees. Prof. Narke wished that he too should be given one 'kafani' for special occasions at least. Baba stopped the distribution in between and said to Narke, "Don't blame Me for not giving you a 'kafani,' The Faqir (God) has not permitted Me to give you one." Thus He gave answer to Prof. Narke's unspoken thoughts.

Narke had studied in England for pretty long time but he could not get a job suited to his qualifications and had to be satisfied with temporary appointments. Whenever he got an offer for a post, he went to Baba to seek permission to go there. If it was Calcutta, He would say, "Go to Calcutta and Poona." If it was Bombay, He would say, "Go to Bombay and Poona." Ultimately he got a suitable job in Poona College. He realized that Baba had foreseen his appointment. In 1916 Narke arrived in Shirdi and learnt that Baba was sending someone to beg on His behalf as He was not well and wished that he should be given that duty. However, Narke dropped the idea and visited Baba in his full suit. Baba said that from then onward Narke should beg on His behalf. For full four months he begged for Baba. He had returned from England, and he was unemployed for a pretty long time, so he had sufficient time to be with Baba. He joined the stream of devotees.

In one of the 'aratis' Baba was in a towering passion. He was fuming, cursing and threatening, whom and what for, nobody could say and the thought occurred to him, "Is Baba mad?" In the evening he was massaging Baba's legs. Then Baba stroking his head said, "Arre Narke, I am not mad." The passing thought which he had in the morning when he was one of the crowds, was known to Him. So he concluded that nothing was concealed from Him.

In 1913, Baba said that Mr. Booty, his father-in-law, would build a stone edifice at Shirdi and Prof. Narke would be in-charge of it. At that time nobody had any idea that Mr. Booty was going to build Bootywada. The idea for that came in 1916. In 1918 after Baba's samadhi this Bootywada became the Samadhi Mandir and Prof. Narke, one of the trustees of the Sansthan, became its in-charge.

Sadashiv Vadhavkar was told by his friend Tamane about Baba's greatness. So both of them went to Shirdi. They hired a tonga from Kopergaon to Shirdi and back from Shirdi to Kopergaon. On the way they purchased mangoes for Baba. When they presented the offerings Baba asked them. "Where are those two mangoes? Why have you kept them there from Me? Bring them to Me." Both the men were dumbfounded at Baba's knowledge and at once brought the mangoes kept in the tonga for themselves. It was about 11a.m. and Sadashiv felt quite hungry since it was his habit to take his day's meal at nine in the morning but he had said nothing about his hunger to anybody. He simply sat like a well-behaved child. In the meanwhile a devotee came with a packet of 'pedhas' (sweetmeats) and placed them before Baba as His 'navaidya'. Baba who usually touched nothing at once picked the packet up, tore it open with his hands and took out a 'pedha' which was rather big in size and threw it at Sadashiv who was then sitting some yards away from Him. Sadashiv thought it was Baba's precious gift that must not be eaten alone. It must be taken home and shared with others. Then Baba seeing that Sadashiv was simply holding the 'pedha' in his hand, instead of eating it, turned to him and said, "It is not given to you for keeping." So, Sadashiv was obliged to eat it. His gnawing hunger was half appeased. After that Baba took up another 'pedha' from the packet and threw it at him which he fancied must be carried to his home to be shared and therefore retained it in his hand but again Baba said to him, "It is not given to you for retention. Eat it." So, he ate that up and his hunger was completely gone. After that Baba did not throw any more 'pedhas' to him nor did He give the remaining 'pedhas' to anybody else. He was fully aware of his gnawing hunger and the half appeased and fully appeased state.

One day, Baba lay stretched beside the wall in the Mosque. The usual time for leaving for Lendi had passed, but He did not move or get up. When He had thus delayed His visit to the Lendi, Sathe and others who were in the Mosque said to Baba, "It is time for you to go to Lendi. Why don't you go?" "My Gajanan is gone," said Baba in a sorrowful voice and did not move from there. Then some one wrote to Shegoon asking how the saint of that place was doing and came to know that the Maharaj had died on the very day Baba had declared him to be dead.

Once, Damu Anna Rasane wrote a letter to consult Baba about a business deal. Before the letter was read out Baba remarked, "What does he write? What is he planning? It seems he is trying to reach for the unattainable." Just because he did not get a favourable reply Dammu Anna came to Shirdi to seek advice personally but could not bring himself to say what he wanted to. At this stage, an unworthy thought crossed his mind. He thought that Baba might agree to the proposal if he was offered a share in the profit. Prompt came the reply to his unspoken thought, "I do not wish to be entangled in something as materialistic as profit sharing. Another time Dammu Anna was planning to buy huge stocks of food grain in the hope of making huge profits. There was no communication but Sai Baba read his thoughts and clearly told him, "Don't do it. You will end up selling at lower rates than you buy." Damu Anna's experiences illustrate how he was saved from actions which would have led to his financial ruin. On another occasion Dammu Anna Rasane was thinking, "There are many crowding to Baba. Do they all derive benefit from Him? Without being questioned Baba said to Rasane, "Look at the mango tree in blossom. If all flowers turned into ripe fruit what a splendid crop it would be! But do they? Most of them fall off as flowers or as unripe fruit owing to winds etc. Very few remain." Once Rasane was thinking. "If Baba were to pass away how hopelessly adrift I would be and how I am to fare then?" To this Baba said that He would be with him whenever he thought of Him, wherever he was.

One day Baba was smoking a chillum and passing it around among those near. One Mr. Kolambe felt a desire to have a puff or two out of that chillum. At once Baba called out to him, "You, boy, come here. Why keep yourself away? Come here and have a puff." Once he was boasting of his immunity from Baba's 'dakshina'. At once, Baba sent a word and demanded two rupees as 'dakshina'. Once a devotee secretly deposited some money with Kolambe so that in case Baba demanded 'dakshina' he could truthfully say that he had no money. And Baba did demand 'dakshina'. At the same time Baba, asked him to take the money from Kolambe and give it to Him. The man's deviousness was obviously found out by Baba.

In 1912, Shanta Ram Balwant Nachane Dhanukar was going to Shirdi. On the way at Kopergaon the station master started a tirade against Baba calling Him a hypnotist who was gulling people. His faith in Baba was shaken to such an extent that he went back without seeing Baba. But after a month, on the persuasion of his sister-in-law, he came to Shirdi. The moment he came in front of Baba, Baba said, "What? You have come without taking leave from the Mamlatdar? (The station master was his boss too.) Don't behave like this again." This removed all the doubts, that the station master's thoughtless remarks, had raised in his mind. He felt he was before a saint who knew every thing that happened even in places far away. The few children who were born to Nachane, died very young. In 1915 when he had gone to Shirdi, his mother-in-law was very anxious that the Nachanes should get Baba's blessings for an issue. So, at Shyama's suggestion Mrs. Nachane offered a coconut to Baba because every woman who wanted a male child came to Baba with a coconut. Baba used to return the coconut to the woman, as an indication that she would bear a child within a year. When Baba was returning the coconut to Mrs. Nachane,

Omniscient Baba

there were tears in His eyes. In fact, nothing was hidden from Him. No doubt, Nachane was blessed with a son but within eighteen months Nachane's wife died. The child Kalu Ram, a mini yogi, died when he was just eight. Destiny could not hide anything from the omniscient Baba.

After the death of Babu, Dada Kalekar's nephew, Mr. Pradhan along with his wife and pregnant sister-in-law went to Shirdi. Pointing at Mrs. Pradhan Baba said, "She is the mother of my Babu." Nana Chandorkar thought that Baba was referring to Mr. Pradhan's sister-in-law who was supposed to be pregnant. Baba categorically said that he meant Chotubai Pradhan. Exactly one year after that Baba sitting at Shirdi was saying that He had labour pains and that twins would be born. One of them would die and the other would survive. This is what happened. Mrs. Pradhan gave birth to twins. One died and the other survived and he got the name Babu.

Once Mrs. Pradhan was performing Baba's puja when He stopped her very abruptly and asked her to go to the Wada as she was needed there very urgently. When she went there she found that her child was crying very loudly and he could not be soothed by any one else. So, she was urgently required in the Wada.

Once Mr. Pradhan wanted to go to Shirdi and the doctor forbade him to take his convalescent baby with him. But the Pradhans did take him with them. In the train he was unwell, he had to lie down and as he could not even sit up. They feared that people would laugh at them. But as soon as they went to Baba the child stood up before Him and Baba said, "People will not laugh now."

Hari Vinayak Sathe had a Brahmin cook named Megha, who was a devotee of Shiva. Sathe sent him to Baba. On the way at the station he came to know that he was being sent to serve a Muslim faqir. He felt distressed. He could not reconcile to the idea of serving a low caste Muslim while he himself was a high caste Brahmin but he had to obey his master. When he reached the Dwarkamai, Baba flew into rage and said, "Kick out that rascal." Pointing His finger at Megha Baba said, "You are a high caste

Brahmin and I am a low caste Muslim. You will lose your caste by coming here." Baba quoted the exact words used by Megha. Megha could not help wondering at Baba's omniscience.

Once he came in contact with Baba, Baba became his Shiva. After worshipping other deities in the village temples, he used to worship Baba with 'bel' leaves and Godawari water, which he used to fetch after walking eight miles. One day the Khandoba Temple was closed so he came to Baba to worship Him but Baba would not let him do so without following the proper procedure. He told him that the Khandoba temple was open then and he could go there. Lo! It was open when Megha went there. Megha could not understand how Baba knew about it when the temple is so far away from the Dwarkamai.

Dr. Mulky was going to Shirdi. On the way at Manmad, the station master started a lecture against Baba. So much so that he started assassinating His moral character. This dissuaded him from proceeding farther. After a month or so when he went to Shirdi, Baba referred to the previous month's incident. He was put to shame and there were tears for even having listened to that scoundrel. Once during his visit to Shirdi, Baba told him that he would find an order on the table, "Transferred to Bijapur on promotion." When he reached home, to his great surprise he found this on the table. He was transferred to Bijapur on promotion.

In 1905 Ramchander Dev alias Balabhat and Krishan Patil wanted to go to Akkalkot Maharaj. Sh. Krishan Patil suggested they should halt at Shirdi as it is on the way. Balabhat had no objection as he had heard a lot about Baba from Das Ganu's 'kirtans' and Amir Sakhar Khatik, a butcher of Bandra, Mumbai. So, he wanted just to see Baba and start off for Akkalkot. When Balabhat saw Baba, Baba said, "I must go to Akkalkot," He was expressing the predominant idea in his mind. He was surprised as Baba expressed his innermost desire. He was so much impressed by this that he prolonged his stay at Shirdi and ultimately stopped going to Akkalkot and started visiting Shirdi frequently.

Omniscient Baba

Hari Sita Ram Dixit was laid up with fever at Shirdi. He was asked to go back home. Rather he was escorted by Shyama. While he was leaving, Baba said to him, "Don't lie down on the bed. Eat almonds, pistachio and 'sheera'. The fever will go in four days" At home, the doctors recommended complete bed rest but Kaka Sahib followed Baba's instructions. Everyone thought that Kaka Sahib would die and started reviling him for pawning his senses to the absurdities of a mad faqir. Later when Kaka Sahib visited Shirdi again, the first question that Baba asked was, "What did your people in Bombay say?"

Once, Mr. Kharparde's financial condition was not good. Baba asked Dixit to give Khaparde two hundred rupees. But He did not insist on the order being carried out as He knew that Khaparde was too proud to accept help.

Baba's knowledge of the future was another aspect of Baba's omniscience. For example in December 1910, Sahastrabudh visited Shirdi. When he bowed to Baba, He said, "Serve Noolkar." Sahastrabudh tried to know the hidden meaning behind these words but could not understand. He was determined not to leave Shirdi before he knew what Baba meant. In the meanwhile, Noolkar fell ill and Sahastrabudh had to look after him in his last days. How prophetic were Baba's words! A little before his death, Noolkar himself said to Sahastrabudh, "Sai did not want me to suffer in my last days. So He has brought you here to serve me."

Cholkar was a poor clerk in Thane. He was unable to support his family. He vowed to Sai Baba that if he got promotion he would go to Shirdi for Baba's 'darshan' and distribute sugar candy. But his financial condition was such that he could not fulfill his vow. So, he started economizing, by taking tea without sugar. As luck would have it he was able to visit Shirdi. When he was about to leave the Dwarkamai for home he was startled to hear Baba tell Bapusahib Jog, "Give this man tea and make sure it is saturated with sugar." These instructions were a clear indication that the secret of the sacrifice Cholkar had made in order to visit Shirdi, was known to Sai Baba.

As per Shyama, the Nimonkars were staying at Shirdi. Their son and daughter-in-law in Poone were attacked by plague. The Nimonkars wanted to go to Poone but Baba would not grant permission. So much so that Mrs. Nimonkar wept because she could not go to look after them. Baba said to her, "Why do you cry? In fifteen days time your son will come." Accordingly, the son and his wife recovered and the son came to Shirdi to see his parents within the period specified by Baba.

Bapusahib Nimonkar's daughter-in-law, Somnath Shankar's wife, was expecting. They were waiting for his parents to come and help at the time of her delivery but Baba at Shirdi would not permit them to go and Somnath Shankar Deshpande had not made any alternate arrangement. One night, at ten the lady had labour pains and was immediately admitted in the hospital. At eleven, while the nurse was still busy talking with Mr. Deshpande the lady delivered a male child. There was no need for assistance. Baba said to Nanasahib Nimonkar at Shirdi, "There was a woman. She was taken to hospital. There she delivered a male child."

In 1912 M. B. Rege went to Shirdi on Guru Purnima day. Other devotees had baskets full of garlands but he had forgotten to bring even one garland. At the Dwarkamai, he was pained still more to see Baba weighed down by garlands. Immediately, omniscient Baba lifted up a bundle of garlands with His hands and said, "All these are yours." In 1915 Mr. Rege bought a beautiful piece of muslin to give Baba, thinking that Baba would look beautiful in it. It was customary for Baba to receive such gifts and return them to the devotees. When Baba was busy in that process, Rege stealthily placed his gift beneath Baba's seat. Baba immediately ordered the seat be dusted. A beautiful muslin piece was found beneath it. Baba hugged it saying, "How fine is the muslin! I shall not return it. It is mine." He put it on and looking at Rege said, "Don't I look beautiful in this?"

It was the time of World War I. M. B. Rege and P. R. Avasthi, a sub judge of Gwalior, were going to Shirdi. At Mhow, all the passengers were asked to get off as the train was needed to transport troops. Rege and Avasthi also had to get down but they prayed to Baba for help. In the meanwhile, the Military Commander came and after inspecting their carriage told them that that compartment was too small to accommodate the troops and that they need not get down. The whole night Avasthi sang devotional songs and prayed to Baba. When they reached Shirdi they went to see Baba who said, "They tried to disembark My children from the train. But I told the captain that they are My children and to let them come to Me. But this Avasthi was by My side the whole night calling Baba! Baba!"

G. K. Rege went to Shirdi after the sad demise of his seven year old son. He took sitaphal (custard apple) and ramphal mangoes from his own garden for Baba. There Baba began to describe to some one present, his house and his garden and the state and the exact number and location of the sitaphal and ramphal trees. with the accuracy and certainty of a neighbour who had actually seen them. He told the others about him and that he had lost his son fifteen days back and thereby removed his poignant grief and fortified his faith in Him by abundant proofs that He knew everything about him. He stayed there for four days. During those days many came to Him. He told them facts which were remarkable proofs of His knowing everything.

Laxmi Chand Jain of Delhi saw a sadhu in his dream. He did not know who that sadhu was. Once he happened to attend Das Ganu's 'kirtan'. There was a photo of Baba. On seeing the photo of Baba, Laxmi Chand Jain felt sure it was Sai Baba of Shirdi who had come in his dream. When he was pining to see Sai Baba, a friend came to his house to enquire if he wanted to accompany him to Shirdi as he was going there. Laxmi Chand Jain was beside himself with joy. He borrowed money from his cousin and left for Shirdi. When he met Baba, Baba's, first question was, "Where was the need to borrow money to come here?" Laxmi Chand Jain's surprise knew no bounds at Baba's omniscience.

There was one more incident which further strengthened his faith in Baba. He had a severe pain in the neck when he went to see

Baba. He did not tell any one anything about it. Baba of his own accord said, "You have a pain in the neck. The necessary medicine for its cure is being prepared. As soon as it is received you take it and the pain will go". Soon a devotee brought semolina pudding for Baba. Laxmi Chand Jain's pain left as soon as he ate it.

Bhikhubai came to Shirdi on the invitation of Radha Krishna Mai, her friend and settled down there. After the sad demise of Radha Krishna Mai she went to Ahmadnagar to collect her family pension. On the way back at Kopergaon she felt very disturbed at the sad demise of her friend. When she went to Baba to offer the garland of flowers, it automatically snapped into three parts and Baba said, "I don't want it." He did not accept the offerings she had brought for Him from Ahmadnagar. Even Dixit requested Baba to eat part of the offering but Baba said, "This woman was shedding tears at the Godawari and she has brought the offerings with a troubled heart and so I will not accept them." The fact is that at the river bank where her friend was cremated she was weeping and blaming Baba mentally for having allowed her friend to die such a wretched death. Baba knew everything that was in her heart and hence his refusal to accept her offerings.

Smt. Kasturibai Kulkarani, a scholar, on hearing about Baba's miracles wondered whether Baba was using black magic. She went to Shirdi to verify this. As soon as she approached the steps of the Dwarkamai Baba came forward and spoke vehemently, "This is a Brahmin. He has nothing to do with black magic. No magician can step into this Brahmin's Masjid. I won't allow any magician to cast his shadow here."

Mr. Samant came to Shirdi to have Baba's 'darshan' and wanted to go back soon. But he could not ask for permission as Baba was in a very furious mood. In no time Baba looked at Samant and said, "Those who want to go can go."

Once, Baba told Appa Kulkarani about the thieves who had entered the village and that they were after important things only. Appa Kulkarani was going to be their first victim. So he was to be careful. So, Appa Kulkarani tightened the security of his property

Omniscient Baba

and strengthened the security staff at his house. But he did not understand Baba's prophecy. He became the first victim of cholera.

A Mumbai devotee, Kaka Mahajani, visited Shirdi with the intention of staying there for a week. "When are you returning home?" was the first question Sai Baba asked on meeting him. Taken aback, he replied that he would go whenever he was told. "Then go tomorrow," Sai Baba ordered him. On his return to Mumbai he discovered that his return was being awaited anxiously by his employer and that a letter asking him to resume work had been mailed to Shirdi, a day earlier. The letter was subsequently redirected to him at Mumbai. The post mark proved that Sai Baba could not have known about it when He issued instructions for Kaka Mahajani to go back.

Narain Moti Ram Jain of Nasik was a devotee of Baba. Baba told his mother that her son should have his own business. Soon, he started a boarding house. Baba's prophecy had came true.

Sh. P Vankiah had kept three five-rupee and three one-rupee notes in a box without his wife's knowledge. On 30th December 1953 Baba appeared in his wife's dream begging for alms. She said that she had no money as her husband had not received his salary. Baba pointed out that there were three five-rupee and three one-rupee notes in a box. In the morning the wife narrated the dream to her husband. At this the husband gave her key of the box and she found the exact amount there.

In 1911, Somdev Swami of Haridwar started for Shirdi to have Baba's 'darshan'. When he reached the Mosque he saw flags fluttering over there. This repelled him. He thought, "Why should a saint have a fancy for flags unless he has a craving for fame?" He wanted to go back. His fellow passengers made him have a look at the saint before he left. Unwillingly, he stepped into the Mosque. On seeing him Baba got wild and yelled, "Go away. Beware if you come back to the Masjid. Why take the 'darshan' of a saint who displays His banners over the Masjid? Is this a sign of sainthood? Get away!" In fact Baba was voicing his earlier feelings. Somdev recognised His omniscience and fell at His feet.

Around 1890 Laxman Govind Munge accompanied by Gadgil and Nimonkar went to see Baba. At night Gadgil set apart some dates, one rupee and a packet of joss sticks for Baba. Nobody else knew about this. Early next morning when they went before Baba, Baba said to Gadgil, "Give me my dates, my joss sticks and my rupee."

Once Dhumal got a portrait of Baba from Radha Krishna Mai and wanted it to be sanctified by Baba. When he was passing by the Mosque, Baba called him and asked him what he was carrying. Baba took the portrait in His hands and then returned it. Dhumal's unexpressed wish was fulfilled.

One day, Baba remarked to devotees about a thorn pricking the foot and losing a parent. Nobody could understand what Baba meant by that. Imam Bhai Chhote Khan, went home and within two days his mother had a thorn stuck in her foot and within a week or so she expired. Then, the devotee knew that the remarks were meant for him. As he had no money after the fourth day he came back to Shirdi and stayed there for thirty-four days and then he heard Baba saying that 'udhi' must be received and leave must be taken. Somehow the devotee felt those words were meant for him. The next morning when he went in front of Baba, He extended His hand with 'udhi' in it, an indication that he was to leave Shirdi. At the time of giving 'udhi' Baba said, "At the doorway of the house, there will be an old woman standing. She will give something, using which celebrations may be performed. Guests have come. The feast should be held in their presence." The devotee could not understsnd what Baba meant by all this. On going home he found the widow of the Kazi standing at his doorway and she gave him fifty rupees and said, "Perform your rituals." That was the fortieth day of his mother's demise. His sisters and his brothers-in-law had come to his place in his absence. These evidently were the guests mentioned by Baba. So he performed the fortieth day rituals with the money given by the old woman. Chhote Khan started visiting Shirdi very frequently. During one of his visits, Baba did not allow him to leave Shirdi. But he was very impatient to go back home.

Omniscient Baba

While refusing permission Baba had said, "People should not go. If they go, there will storms and balls of fire and immense trouble." This was spoken by Baba talking in general as was His habit. It did not appear to refer to Chote Khan. So he started the journey. He travelled at a speed of 5–6 miles an hour and had covered 10–12 miles. On the way, at 5:30 pm the Patil of that village told him not to proceed as the weather was very tricky. But he did not pay heed to it. When he had covered 3 miles more, there came a big storm and lightning fell on a huge tree close by in front of him. The tree crashed and broke into two and a fire started in the tree. He was dazed by the lightning and turned his face away from it. Then there was a river near the village. He felt that the water was knee deep but when he reached the other shore and looked back, he saw the river was in full flood and was amazed, as water was over flowing its banks. The depth of the river might have been 20 feet! Baba's statement about a storm and balls of fire proved to be correct. Once Baba said, "Gulab (rose) has come." When he went home he found that his wife had given birth to a child. He named the child Gulab.

One day, a certain devotee was pressing Baba's feet. Suddenly Sai Baba ordered him to stop. He felt dejected and appealed to Baba with tears in his eyes to accept his service. But it was of no use. At first, he could not understand why Baba had so suddenly refused to accepot his service. But on closer introspection, he realized that some unworthy thought had passed his mind at that moment and so Baba was responding to it.

Kashi Ram, a cloth merchant, was a devotee of Baba. Once he was waylaid by robbers. While Kashi Ram was struggling with the dacoits Sai Baba at Shirdi was vociferously abusing in anger, looking in the direction where Kashi Ram was. Devotees nearby at once felt that some devotee of Sai Baba must be in danger and all this anger and fighting was meant to fight for and avert the danger to his devotee, a phenomenon, which ultimately, proved to be true.

Once Noolkar, a sub-judge of Pandharpur, was unwell. As a rule he should have got himself treated by some good doctor.

But instead of that he went to Shirdi Sai Baba for treatment. This prompted criticism among the lawyers over there. Among those lawyers, the most prominent was Septnaker, who made fun of Baba. After a decade or so, after the untimely demise of his only son he went to Shirdi in search of peace. When he reached the Dwarkamai, he observed all the formalities which a devotee is expected to observe. When Baba saw all this He remarked, "How cunning some people are! They bow before you, offer you 'dakshina' but behind your back they say foul things." Septnaker admitted that those remarks were meant for him. Omniscient Baba knew what had happened years back at Pandharpur.

Mr. Joshi of Thane, was angry with Baba as all the members of his house had left for Shirdi and he was the only one left behind. He wanted Baba to prove that He was God. When a Konkani gentleman with his family was returning, Baba gave him a packet of 'udhi' to be given at Thane, to a man who requested him for space to sit. The gentleman promised to do the allotted work but in case he could not meet the gentleman he said he would write to Baba. He thought that the train had passed Thane and so, here was no chance of meeting the gentleman. He took out a postcard to write to Baba. To his surprise, the train stopped at Thane. In came a man who asked him to take his child on his lap as he was feeling giddy and he wanted to sit. The Konkani gentleman immediately offered him space to sit down and the packet of 'udhi' which Baba had sent for the gentleman who requested for the place to sit. Baba's angry devotee was fully satisfied.

Hari Khandoba of Bombay came to Shirdi to test Baba's divinity. He put on his best dress, the best turban and the best shoes. When he entered the Dwarkamai he had to leave his shoes outside. All the time he was in the Dwarkamai his mind was on the new footwear he had left outside. When he came out of the Dwarkamai, he was shocked to find his shoes missing. Barefooted he went back to his room. As he was taking his meals, there came a boy with a pair of shoes on a stick and he was shouting, "Hari ka beta, zari ka feta". (Hari's son with a turban of zari) Hari Khandoba came out to see who was shouting his name. He was surprised to find his shoes on a stick. He was told that Baba had sent the boy to give those shoes to the man who responded to this announcement. He showed the boy his 'zari' headgear and got his shoes back. He thought Baba could have known his name and might have seen his 'zari' turban but how could He know his father's name?. Baba had passed the test. His divinity could not be doubted.

A man staying at Bandra was leaving for office. His wife asked him for a rupee which the man thought he did not have. So he promised to give it in the evening when he came back home. While searching for a handkerchief he found a one-rupee coin in his pocket but did not have the courtesy to go back and give it to his wife. In the evening when he returned he handed over a rupee to his wife. A few days after that, the couple went to Shirdi. No sooner did they bow before Baba than Baba remarked to the wife, "Mother, now-a-days some one has become so untruthful that there was a rupee in his pocket but he said there was none. The lady was unperturbed as she knew nothing about the incident but the husband could recollect it in no time. He fell at Baba's feet and apologized.

Udhvesh of Dahanu was going to Dwarka by steamer. On the way his purse slipped into the sea. He had no money. He wrote to Baba for money. Before the letter reached Shirdi, Baba appeared twice in the dream of Girdhar Gopal and forced him to send money to Dwarka. As Udhvesh of Dahanu was at Dwarka at that time he sent a money order in the name of Udhvesh. When Udhvesh went to Shirdi, Baba immediately remarked, "I had money sent to you."

Anwar Khan Kazi wanted to rebuild a mosque. He came to Baba for funds. Baba told him that the mosque would not accept any money from any one. It would provide the funds itself. He said to him, "Dig three feet under the nimber and you will find a treasure. Re-build the mosque with that." Baba's words came true. The masjid did provide funds itself.

Once in the presence of a Goan gentleman Baba started telling a story in the first person of how He had travelled by ship and how He lost 30,000 rupees. Shyama felt that it was all a bluff as Baba had never been beyond Rahata and Neemgaon. Moreover Baba never had so much money. But the Goan gentleman said that He was telling his story. He was really surprised as to how He had quoted the exact amount.

Swami Sharan Anand left an empty compass box for Baba at Radha Krishna Mai's house beneath her cupboard without informing any one else. At Mumbai, Swami Sharan Anand came to know that Baba got Radha Krishna Mai's house searched for the box. To her surprise, she found the box and gave it to Baba.

Dattatrey Vithal says that he was with his father at Shirdi. His father was anxious to leave Shirdi to join duty in time but Baba delayed permission by four hours. When the permission was granted, it seemed futile to go to the station as the train by which they were to travel, would have left and there was no other train. As per tradition, once the permission was granted they could not stay back in Shirdi. So, they had to leave for the station. To their pleasant surprise the train by which they were to leave was late by 5 hours! And it arrived at the station after they reached there. They were benefitted by Baba's omniscience and left by the scheduled train.

In 1913, Hari Bhau M Phanse had been convicted for misappropriation and sentenced to imprisonment. He had been let out on bail pending his appeal. As Balwant Nachane was going to Shirdi, he said to him, "Tell Baba that I am in trouble and that I am innocent." Before Nachane could convey the message, Baba Himself said, "Tell him that he need not have any anxiety and that he shall be acquitted in the appeal." When Nachane returned and conveyed the message Phanse told him that he had already been acquitted.

A police officer went to Baba. Baba asked him for 'dakshina'. The officer replied that he had nothing. Baba then said "See your purse. There is a fifty-rupee note in it." The note was then produced

Omniscient Baba

and offered to Baba. But Baba wanted only a small amount out of it and told him to keep the balance as he would soon be in trouble and need it. So indeed it happened. Soon after this visit, the officer got into trouble and had to use that balance to extricate himself.

In 1909, at Kopergaon a lady took a loan of ten rupees from Kashi Ram Dubey and promised to return it when she came back from Aurangabad and at the same time she talked of Shirdi Sai Baba. Kashi Ram had heard the name of Sai Baba for the first time. As he was doubtful that he would get the money back, he decided to offer it to Sai Baba in case he got the loan back. As luck would have it, he got the money back and went to Shirdi. There Baba pestered him for 'dakshina.' At first he gave five rupees, then two rupees then two rupees more and then one rupee. After that Baba did not pester him for more 'dakshina'. Baba had received the promised amount.

Anpurnabai Daji Bhave went to Shirdi. There when she tried to enter the Dwarkamai Baba prevented her saying that it would pollute the place. In fact, when she was on pilgrimage her daughter-in-law had expired and she was in the 10 day period when the bereaved family does not enter places of worship. She did not know this but omniscient Baba knew it.

Kharparde says that on 8th December 1910 a head constable came to Shirdi. He was charged with extracting money. He vowed to visit Sai Baba if he was acquitted. And he was acquitted. So he came to Shirdi to honour his vow. On seeing him Sai Baba said, "Why did you not stay a few days more there? The people must have felt disappointed." He repeated this twice. Afterwards it was learnt that this gentleman's friends had pressed him to stay and that he did not comply with their request. He had never seen Sai Baba before and, of course, the latter could not have seen Him before. The wonder is how Sai Baba knew him and had said what he said.

Baba knew what was happening even in the minds of creatures other than human beings also. One day a lizard on the wall was making a tick-tick sound. A devotee asked Baba whether the sound produced by the lizard was of any particular signifiance. "The lizard is happy because her sister is coming to see her from Aurangabad," Baba told him. The explanation perplexed the devotee but he kept quiet. Minutes later a gentleman from Aurangabad stopped at the Mosque to see Sai Baba. He had come on horseback and had broken his journey at Shirdi as the horse was hungry. The man unslung a cloth bag containing feed for the horse and thumped it to rid it of dust. A lizard made its way up the wall to the other lizard and the two went scuttling along.

One day when Baba was sitting in the Mosque, he suddenly exclaimed in pain, "Oh! They are killing him. Go quickly and fetch him." In fact, a trainer had been engaged to train Shyam Karan, Baba's favourite horse, but he had been beating him.

V S Joshi sent ten rupees as 'dakshina' through a friend who was going to Shirdi and requested him to take a photograph of Baba. The friend gave the 'dakshina' but did not have the courage to take the photograph. After a few minutes, Baba suddenly told the gentleman to take His photograph. The latter took two photographs of Baba. one in a sitting posture and the other in a standing posture.

In 1918, on the eve of Ram Naumi 'namsaptah' (non-stop chanting of the divine name of Rama for seven days) was going on. Several devotees were seated in the Dwarkamai. Baba called Shyama and said, "Go out and fetch the candy which the old man has brought for Me." Shyama went out and found a very old man standing there. He looked senile owing to age. Sliva was dripping from his parted lips and flies were swarming all over his face. Shyama led the old man by the hand into Baba's presence. Baba then kept His hand on the old man's head in blessing, took a little candy from the small bundle in his garment and gave the rest to him as 'prasad'.

In December 1915, one Balaram Mankar went to the Tarkhands and told them that he was going to Shirdi and asked them whether they had any message for Baba. Mrs. Tarkhand (Mrs. Manager) wanted to send some gift to Baba. She searched the whole house but found nothing but a 'pedha' (milk cake) which had already been offered to Sai Baba's picture in the shrine. Generally such a thing is considered unworthy of being offered a second time. But she hoped that Baba would care more for her love than for the thing sent. Balaram was in the period of mourning consequent upon the death of his father and such a person is usually considered impure to carry such a holy gift. Anyway, Balaram took the 'pedha' with him to Shirdi but in his hurry to see Sai Baba, forgot to take it to Him. Baba waited for him to recollect it. When Balaram visited Baba in the afternoon, he again forgot to take it. Now Baba's patience gave way. He said, "What did you bring for Me from Bandra?" "Nothing" said Balaram. Baba repeated His question a little later but got the same reply. At last Baba said, "Didn't the mother Tarkhand give you some sweetmeat for Me?" Now the young man remembered the whole thing and brought the 'pedha'. Baba eagerly received it and ate it at once. All the love and devotion of the lady was fully reciprocated.

6

Image Worship

Baba used to say that there is no difference between His physical self and His image. Worshipping the image is worshipping Baba and He proved it on a number of occasions.

Balabua Sutar of Bombay was a famous saint, who by his melodious 'bhajans,' had earned the title of modern Tukaram. He came to Shirdi for the first time in 1917 and bowed before Baba. Baba said to the people gathered there, "I know this man for the last four years." This puzzled Sutar but then he remembered that he had prostrated to a picture of Baba in Bombay exactly four years back and it was that Baba was alluding to.

Baba once came to Hemadpant in a vision and told him that he would be coming for lunch that full moon day. In an extraordinary chain of events a picture of Baba was unexpectedly delivered to Hemadpant's house just as the midday meal was about to start.

Once when bathing Sai Baba's statue, one of the priests dropped a container on it but did not attach any importance to it. For the next two days he had a severe pain in his knee. He went to the doctor, had injections, took painkillers and did every thing he could to alleviate the pain but to no effect. Eventually he prayed to Baba and asked Him why he had to suffer in this way. That night Baba came to him in a dream and said, " You think you are in pain but how do you think I felt when you dropped the container on Me?" Thereafter the priest was careful not to hurt Baba in any way and respected the idol as if it were the living Baba.

Image Worship

Balasahib Tarkhand of Bombay was a Prarthna Samajist. His wife, popularly known as Mrs. Manager (because her husband was a mill manager) and her son were ardent devotees of Sai Baba. Once during the summer vacation Master Tarkhand was asked to accompany his mother to Shirdi but he was reluctant to go because his daily worship of Baba's photograph at home would suffer. His father being a Samajist might not care to worship it in his absence. Knowing his fears, Mr. Tarkhand solemnly promised him that he would conduct the daily worship on his behalf. Mrs. Tarkhand left for Shirdi on a Friday night after her husband promised to conduct the daily workship. During the next three days Mr. Tarkhand performed the worship scrupulously. Every day he offered sugar as 'navaidya' to Baba's photograph and the same was distributed to all at lunch time. On Tuesday, he conducted the worship and rushed to his office to reach in time. He forgot to offer 'navaidya' to Baba's picture that day. Later Tarkhand was shocked at this grave lapse. After lunch he wrote a letter to his son at Shirdi confessing his lapse, praying for Baba's forgiveness and promising that he would not repeat the error. The same day (i.e. Tuesday) at Shirdi Sai Baba said to Mrs. Tarkhand, "Mother, I was very hungry. I went to your home at Bandra hoping to find something to eat. I found the door locked yet I managed to enter the room. But I found that Bhau (Mr. Tarkhand) had not left anything for Me to eat. So I have returned unappeased." The lady could not understand His words. But Master Tarkhand, at once, realized that there was some error in his father's worship at Bandra. After the noon 'arati' Master Tarkhand promptly wrote a letter to his father conveying to him Baba's words and requesting him to see that there was no lapse in the worship. The father's letter reached the son and the son's letter reached the father at the same time. Thus, the physical identity of Baba with His picture was established.

A theft took place in the house of a man. His wife's jewellery box was gone. The thief was none other than a close friend of the man. He could not even report it to the police. He just sat in front of Baba's photo and wept. The very next day the errant friend turned up to return the jewellery box and to beg forgiveness.

A friend of Dr. Rajgopalachari presented him a picture of Baba. He got it framed and fixed on the wall and forgot about it. One night, a faqir with boils on his legs appeared in his dream. The next morning, he casually glanced at Baba's photo and noticed that He was the faqir of his dream. Baba's picture was destroyed by white ant upto the legs. The doctor realized that Sai Baba is one with His picture and started worshipping Him.

One day Sai Baba who was sitting in His usual place in the Mosque suddenly bawled out "Oh!" for no apparent reason. The next moment His head-dress and His 'kafani' were suddenly found drenched with water and water was dripping from them for more than an hour. The little space in the Dwarkamai became a pool of water. The devotees were amazed and silently swept out the water. Neither Baba told them anything about it nor had they the boldness to ask Him. On the third day, Baba received a telegram from one of His devotees, Jahangir Premji, who offered his thanks to Baba for saving him.

Russo-Japanese war was in its bitterest phase. This devotee was the captain of a ship. When he found that all his steamers except three were sunk by the enemy and the rest of them including his own would meet the same fate, he took out Baba's photograph from his pocket and with tears in his eyes prayed to Baba to save him and his three steamers. Baba at once appeared on the scene and towed all the sinking steamers to the bank.

Sh. Daleep Kumar Roy of Poona was a famous disciple of Shri Aurobindo and a great devotee of Lord Krishna. He established the Hare Krishna Ashram in Poona and was leading several seekers on the path of devotion. Somewhere around 1970, a friend of Daleep Kumar Roy presented him with an idol of Sai Baba. Sh. D K Roy kept it, along with several other idols in an open place in the Ashram compound. That night, Sai Baba appeared before him and said, " I am shivering in the cold. Take Me inside the Ashram

Image Worship

and keep Me in a comfortable place." Soon Sh. Roy kept the idol of Baba inside the Ashram and later kept it in a small shrine.

Ganesha is a deity fond of food and Baba identified Himself with him. Heartfelt offerings and worship rendered even to an inanimate lifeless idol in the true spirit of devotion and faith, are sure to reach the spirit which pervades all saints, animals and even idols.

It is the spirit behind the worship that is of prime importance. Hence Baba did not condemn idol worship. It is a valid form of spiritual practice, for those who are by nature made for it.

7

Baba's Miracles

*B*aba never used miracles as visiting cards. He performed all his miracles for the protection and welfare of His people. This continues to happen with countless devotees throughout the world even today. To people who earnestly remember Him in the hour of their need, He instantly provides His miraculous help. Sometimes He appears in His usual form or in the form of any other saint, beggar, unknown person or creature, but the earnest devotee is certainly able to recognize Him when His grace falls on him/her. Innumerable books and journals published by Sai devotees throughout the world are overflowing with the accounts of many such thrilling miracles of Baba in the post samadhi period.

At the age of sixteen, on the last day at His guru's ashram, Baba performed a thrilling miracle of bringing back to life the dead body of His ashram mate who had tried to hit Him with a brick on the forehead and who had then suddenly died.

Another occasion when Baba revived a dead person was, in the Chawadi. Malabai suffered from TB. When all medical aid failed to cure her, she insisted that she be taken to Shirdi. When she was brought to Shirdi, Baba asked her to lie down on a blanket and take nothing but water. She carefully followed all His instructions but died. At that time Baba was in the Chawadi. The girl's parents were making preparations for the funeral when suddenly they saw that the girl was breathing. She opened her eyes and looked around. She told them that a black person was carrying her away. Terribly frightened, she had cried to Baba for help. Baba took His staff and gave that black person a good beating. He snatched her away from the black figure and carried her to the Chawadi. She had not seen the Chawadi before but she gave a correct description of it. Just then, Baba left the Chawadi and came to the place where the girl's body had been kept.

After the brick incident, Guru Venkusa transferred all his powers to Baba. He asked Baba to bring a black cow's milk. The cow that Baba could bring was barren. Guru Venkusa passed his hand from the head to the tail of the cow and then said that the cow should be milked. To the surprise of all present, the cow yielded copious milk.

Just a few days before his second move to Shirdi in 1858, Baba performed three miracles before Chand Patil in the forest, making a live ember and water for his chillum materialize and then showing him his lost mare grazing near a stream.

Dass Ganu wanted to go to Prayag to have a dip in the holy water of the Sangam. Baba materialized holy water from His toes for him.

Baba used to beg oil from local merchants to light lamps in the Masjid. One evening, the shopkeepers played a prank. They refused to oblige Him and said that they had run out of stock. Unruffled, Baba came back with the empty tin. He put some water into it and lighted the lamps, which burnt brightly the whole night! The miracle of the lamps opened the eyes of the people of Shirdi. Balkrishan Ram Chander Khaikar and Chander Bai Borkar both saw Baba filling lamps with water instead of oil and drinking the remnants of oil mixed with water.

A blind man asked Baba for eyesight for a short while to see only Him and then to take it back. Baba granted his request. He was able to see Baba in human form and then he lost his eyesight again. Swami Sharananand has reported about a blind man whom he saw during Baba's time in Shirdi but who was found reading religious books in 1942–43! Evidently he had regained his eyesight through Baba's grace.

In 1916 Baba restored Vithal Rao Deshmukh's grandfather's eyesight.

In 1915 Abdul Kadir begged Baba to give him 'faqiri' as he wanted to become a saint. Baba stretched out His folded palm at him as though He held something in it. There was nothing visibly held in Baba's hand. But thereafter Kadir started behaving like Baba.

In 1886, Baba announced that He would go into meditation for three days. It was to rid himself of an attack of asthma. Mhalsapathy was to protect his body during that period. Baba's breathing stopped. There was no heartbeat or pulse. He was declared dead. His body was either to be cremated or buried within twenty-four hours but Mhalsapathy would not let anybody touch Baba's body. At the end of three days, Baba came back to life! It was a miracle, which opened the eyes of the people of Shirdi who thought that Baba was only a mad faqir.

During Baba's time, there were two wells in Shirdi. One was completely dry and the water in the other was brackish. The villagers came to Baba and told Him of this problem. Baba turned the brackish water in the well into sweet water by throwing flowers into it.

A Christian Income Tax Officer was sent to assess Baba's income. It was believed His income exceeded that of a governor. His report was that Baba distributed hundreds of rupees per day while he received much less. He attributed this to some divine power. Hence there was no tax on Baba.

One story about Baba was that when He washed Himself He vomited out His intestines, cleaned them and swallowed them again. Shivamma Thayee had also seen Baba taking his intestines out, washing them, spreading them on the walls of the well and then swallowing them again.

There are written records of two persons who saw Baba perform Khandyog. Once a gentleman went towards the Mosque and saw Sai Baba's limbs scattered here and there. He was so terrified that his first impulse was to inform the authorities that Baba had been murdered but he refrained from doing so as he thought he himself might be considered the culprit.

In 1915, Shivamma Thayee (twenty-three or twenty-four-year-old then) witnessed a very horrible sight. She was staying in a rented room very close to the Dwarkamai. There was no toilet in that house. One night at 1.30 a.m. she wanted to relieve herself and for that she had to cross the Dwarkamai. As she walked near the Masjid something like a wooden leg struck her foot. She picked it up. To her horror, it was the leg of a human being with blood! She immediately put it down. After going only about five or six feet, she hit upon another mutilated part of the human body. It was an arm cut off from the shoulder. Walking farther, a distance of four or five feet, she found another leg. She was terribly frightened. At once she ran back to her bedroom and closed the door. The thought that came into her mind was that someone had murdered Sai Baba and mutilated His limbs and thrown them in the street near the Masjid. In the morning, the police would come to investigate and there would be a lot of hue and cry in the village. After that, she could not sleep at all and kept crying the whole night. At 5 a.m., she got up from the bed and mustered courage to peep through the window of her room. To her pleasant surprise, she saw Baba sitting in the open courtyard and smoking His chillum. She went to Baba and narrated to Him her hair-raising experience of the night in a choked voice. Baba then said to Shivamma Thayee, "Daughter Shivamma, I had done my Khandyog last night. I do it sometimes. I separate my limbs from my body and then my physical self is no more there. My spirit saw you moving in the street and stumbling against My mutilated legs and hands but I did not speak to you because firstly My physical body was dead and My limbs lay scattered, and secondly, although My spirit was mutely observing your movements in the street I could not talk to you. I chose not to give you any assurance or sign of My presence there lest you should be frightened in the pitch-dark night."

Narsimha Swami wanted to do Sai 'Prachar' throughout the length and breadth of the country but he had no resources. He wondered where to go for money. The miracle of miracles! A South Indian merchant came to him and left Rs. 11,500 with him for Sai Prachar.

Is death transferable? Of course not. But Baba could do it. Tatya was to die in 1918. Baba gave up his life to save Tatya as a debt to the latter's mother who used to feed Baba at a time when he was just a mad faqir in people's eyes.

13 July 1961 was the darkest day for the people of Pune as Panchat dam burst and drowned Pune. Bungalows and buildings collapsed like a pack of cards. But it was nothing short of a miracle to see the Sai temple (only four by five feet tall) standing intact.

Mrs Chander Bai Borkar also saw Baba lying on a plank hung up from the ceiling with strings made of slender shreds of cloth. There were lamps on the plank on which He lay.

8

Baba's Teachings

As far as Sai Baba's style of teaching is concerned, He never delivered sermons. He made the minimum use of language. In fact, most of what was conveyed was something which words cannot describe. His whole way of living was a continuous lesson of perfect humility, purity, self-control, equality and generosity.

Evils of Lust

Baba's omniscient gaze was watchful of His devotees' conduct and if ever He discovered that any of them was committing a folly, He was prompt in his correction.

An opportunity occurred to Chandorkar to learn about the evils of lust. Once he was sitting in the Dwarkamai. Two Muslim women came for Baba's darshan. Chandorkar was smitten by the beauty of the younger one. He thought, "Shall I have another opportunity to see this angelic face?" Baba instantly slapped his thigh and he knew it for certain that it was for his low and unfit thoughts.

On another occasion, Baba saved H.V. Sathe when he was going to bed with a prostitute. Baba flung open the door and an ashamed Mr Sathe immediately left the place, never to go there again.

Labour to be Rewarded

Baba gave a princely sum of two rupees to a person who had just brought a ladder. It was to teach that nobody should take others' labour free and that the worker should be rewarded immediately and promptly.

No Backbiting

Once a devotee was wasting his precious time in criticizing one of his acquaintances behind his back. A little later, the devotee met Baba, who pointed to a pig on the wayside and said, "See with what gusto it is gorging on the night soil. Your conduct was similar. You go on reviling your own brethren to your heart's content. You have obtained a human birth as a result of much merit in your past life. But if you behave like this, what can a trip to Shirdi do for you?"

Exemplary Patience

Baba taught patience through an example. Once a crazy sadhu named Nanavali came and said to Baba, "Get up. I want to sit on your seat." Baba quietly vacated the seat and the impertinent sadhu occupied it. After a few minutes the sadhu realized his mistake, got down from the seat and fell at Baba's feet. He requested Baba to occupy the seat. The point to note is that Baba never lost patience throughout the whole process.

Humility

Once, Mrs Manager was sitting next to Baba. A foul-smelling leper came for Baba's darshan. He took time to climb the steps and she, felt the stench so intensely, that she hoped he would go soon. At last when he went away, carrying a dirty parcel in his hand, she thanked God for that. Baba darted a piercing glance at her and sent someone to fetch that leper back. Baba took the parcel from the leper. It contained pedas. Of all the people sitting in the Dwarkamai, He gave one piece to her to eat! The omniscient Baba had read her thoughts and he taught her a lesson of humility.

Control over Passions

Ramdasi was an ill-tempered man though he was a regular reader of the *Vishnu Sahastranam*. Baba wanted to correct this flaw in his nature. He sent him away and gave his book to Shama who did not even know Sanskrit. Ramdasi thought that Shama had stolen his book and so he flared up. At this Baba said, "What is the fun in reading the *Vishnu Sahastranam* when you are not able to control your passions? Moreover, you have memorized it. You don't need it." Ramdasi at once understood what Baba wanted to convey.

No Ego

Bayaji Appaji Patel boasted that he had the strength of Bhim. He would lift Baba, carry Him to the dhuni and drop Him there. Baba wanted to teach him a lesson. One day, when he tried to lift Baba to carry Him to the dhuni, he discovered to his dismay that he could not. Baba looked at him and laughed. That laughter was a rebuke against his ego.

On another occasion Baba punctured the ego of Chandorkar, who believed himself to be a great Sanskrit scholar. Once when he was mumbling a sloka, Baba asked him to explain it to Him, word for word, which Chandorkar could not. Instead Baba explained the sloka to him in detail.

9

Baba's Gravitational Pull

Sai Baba was a grand player who drew different birds, big and small, in varied colours from various parts, tying silken strings and some times nylon ropes to their legs which were at times visible and at times, not. Some flocked to Baba having heard about His divine powers from others like Nana Sahib Chandorkar and Das Ganu who had seen or tasted them to their hearts' content and some ran to Him because their parents-in-law had gone to Baba. Some went there to scoff and scorn. But when they came, they saw and surrendered. To some birds He assumed the form of another person and snatched them to Him even before they knew who He was. Sometimes He went in person in their dreams and visions and pulled them to Him to shower on them His love and grace.

In others words, Sai Baba used to say, "I draw My man to Me wherever and however far he might be like a bird with a string tied to its legs." How true it was in the case of Kaka Sahib Dixit, a famous lawyer of Bombay. In 1906 Mr. Dixit met with an accident and developed a limp in one of his legs. He developed an inferiority complex. In 1909, he met his friend Chandorkar and told him about his mental condition and for that Chandorkar recommended Sai Baba of Shirdi. In the meanwhile, Mr. Dixit went to Ahmadnagar. From there he wanted to proceed to Shirdi. Mr. Dixit's host was thinking of a proper person who could escort Mr. Dixit to Shirdi. At the same time Baba was making His own arrangement to draw His devotee to Him in His mysterious manner. Shyama had to go to

Baba's Gravitational Pull

Ahmadnagar to see his ailing mother-in-law. There he happened to meet Mr, Dixit's host. Who could be a better escort than Shyama? Mr. Dixit reached Shirdi without any difficulty. On his arrival Baba said that He was waiting for him. He had purposely sent Shyama to bring him to Shirdi.

Kakaji Vaidya, the priest in the temple of goddess Saptshringi at Vani, had a series of calamities in life. He had lost peace of mind. So he prayed to the Goddess to help him. One night, the goddess appeared in his dream and told him to go to Baba. The priest thought that she had directed him to Shiva, the Bhole Baba. He went to Trembkeshwar and spent ten days there but to no effect. He was as restless as ever. Again, he prayed to the Goddess for help. This time the goddess said, "By Baba I meant Sai Baba of Shirdi. Go there." Kakaji did not know where Shirdi was and how to go there and none could guide him. Baba's omniscient gaze noticed the bird's longing and His invisible hand promptly arranged what the situation needed.

Shyama had fallen ill when he was a child. His mother vowed to take him to the Septshringi if he got well. But she forgot her vow. After sometime she had some skin problem on the breasts and vowed to offer silver breasts when she got cured. But till her death, she could not honour her vows. On her death bed, she told Shyama about her vows and expected him to visit the Goddess on her behalf. For thirty long years Shyama forgot all about this. At this juncture, there came an astrologer who reminded him of his vows. Shyama immediately got made silver breasts and offered them to Baba as Baba was everything to him. Baba refused to accept the offering as He was not at Shirdi when the vows were made. So Shyama had to go to Septshringi at Vani. Shyama arrived at Kakaji's house. The priest was thrilled to know that a man from Shirdi had come precisely at a moment when he himself was dying to know where Shirdi was. There was no need to tell Baba about his sufferings. The sight of Sai Baba made his mind calm and composed. After ten days he returned to Vani but his heart was in Baba's possession.

Once Ram Lal, a Panjabi Brahmin of Bombay, had a dream in which he saw a saint who asked him to come to Shirdi. The saint's spiritual magnetism was so great that he wanted to have His 'darshans' but he did not know His whereabouts. The next day, when he was walking along a street he saw the portrait of a holy man in a shop. The features of the saint in that picture tallied with those of the saint in his dream. He made enquiries from the shopkeeper and came to know that He was Sai Baba of Shirdi. Soon after that he went to Shirdi and stayed there till his death.

Nana Sahib Chandorkar talked of Baba's greatness to Tatya Sahib Noolkar and advised him to visit Shirdi. Mr. Noolkar put two conditions to test to Baba' grace. He said he would go there if he could get a Brahmin cook and good oranges to offer to Sai Baba. In the meanwhile there came a Brahmin cook seeking employment at Chandorkar's place. He directed him to Mr. Noolkar who realized that his one condition was fulfilled. Shortly after that Noolkar received a parcel of hundred oranges as a gift from Nagpur. The sender was mysteriously unknown. Now nothing could hold him back from rushing to Shirdi

A sickly looking clerk, Ganesh Gopal, who earned only fifteen rupees per month, wanted to go to Shirdi but could not afford it. A party was leaving for Shirdi. He went to the station to send some flowers for Baba through that party. As one member of the party could not go, there was a spare ticket and that ticket was offered to Ganesh Gopal. Baba had made arrangements for him.

Mr. Chandorkar, the District Collector of Ahmadnagar, was sent for twice by Baba but he considered it below his dignity to go to meet a Muslim 'faqir' living in an old dilapidated mosque of a small village like Shirdi. There were entreaties from his subordinate Das Ganu to seek blessings for his barren daughter and on the other hand, there was pressure from his boss to go to Shirdi to convince the people to get inoculated against diseases. Nana Sahib had to come to Shirdi. Baba managed the situation in such a manner that he could neither suppress his love for his daughter nor defy the orders of his boss.

One night in October 1910 Lala Laxmichand Jain, a clerk in a Mumbai office, had a strange dream. He saw a bearded old man standing surrounded by His devotees. Later at Das Ganu's 'kirtan' at his house, he recognized in Baba's portrait displayed there, the saint who had appeared in his dream. Hearing about Baba's powers, he decided to visit Shirdi at the earliest. The same day at 8 p.m. his friend Shankar Rao called on him and asked him if he would accompany him to Shirdi. His joy knew no bounds. He borrowed Rs. 15 from his cousin and started for Shirdi. Along the way the two pilgrims did 'bhajan' for some time and then meeting some Muslims who lived near Shirdi enquired of them about Baba. When they saw Baba at the Masjid, looking at Laxmichand Jain He said, "What a cunning fellow! He does 'bhajan on the way and yet enquires from others about Me. Why ask others? We must see everything for ourselves. Just see whether your dream has come true or not. But why borrow money from a Marwadi friend for this trip? Are you now satisfied?" A chain of mysterious co-incidences ultimately proved to be the deliberate design of the saint to get His devotee to Him.

R B Purandhar says that Baba appeared in his dream and called him to Shirdi. At that time his elder daughter then aged six months, was very ill and so his mother objected to his going. Still he went to Shirdi with the ailing child, and stayed there for thirteen days.

Nanu Bhatt Pujari says that in 1914 when he was at Sangamner Baba appeared in his dream and said. "Boy, why are you sleeping? Do not stop here. Come to Shirdi. There is plenty of fun at Shirdi." Baba had already made arrangements for him. His sister's father-in-law came to their place the very next day. He was going to Shirdi. He invited him to accompany him to Shirdi to assist him. So there was no hurdle. He had to accompany him to Shirdi.

Once a theft took place in the house of a Goan gentleman. The thief was their servant who had worked with the family for over thirty-five years. He spent five days crying and weeping over the loss of Rs. 30,000. Then, on the fifth day a Faqir came to him. He told him to forgo his favourite food till he got his money back and then go to Shirdi Sai Baba. He did as he was directed. In a fortnight's time, his servant came back and returned the money. He was so happy that he forgot his vow to visit Shirdi. Baba would not let him go like this. He appeared in his dream and reminded him of his vow and so the gentleman could not help visiting Shirdi. He had to.

It was in the first week of May 1910, Moreshwar Pradhan's brother and other relatives were having a chat with Nana Sahib Chandorkar, a family friend. When Ramarao Moreshwar Pradhan's brother casually asked Chandorkar whether they could ever see or meet another man of the type and order of Akkalkot Maharaj. Nana asked Ramarao if he really wanted to meet such a man. Ramarao said he did. Nana told him to go to Shirdi and see such a man in Sai Baba. Ramarao said it was the first time he had ever heard of Shirdi and of Sai Baba and asked him where Shirdi was and how one could go to that place. So, Chandorkar gave him the details of the route to Shirdi and a vivid and glowing account of the incredible wonders of Baba. This made such a powerful impression on all his listeners that the very next day all of them left for Shirdi in a group of fourteen persons to see the saint for themselves.

When the party left for Shirdi. Mr. Pradhan was out of station. When the party returned Mr. Pradhan borrowed from his brother a photo of Baba and a book containing information about Baba, promising to return them by the next day. Mr. Pradhan read out the book aloud to his wife. After reading the book Pradhan's doubts and misgivings about Baba were gone. He was sure that Baba was a genuine saint. The effect on Mrs. Pradhan was still deeper. She could not think of returning the book and the photo on a Thursday. They returned the articles after three days only when Ramarao asked for them. They had developed a burning desire to go to Shirdi but could not proceed as Mr. Pradhan's recently widowed pregnant sister-in-law could not be left alone. The delivery could take place anytime and he was the only male member there to take care of her. Somehow, Mr. Pradhan, along with Mr. Chandorkar's sons, left for Shirdi within a week or so. When he was face to face with Baba, he found Him a divine saint. He thanked God that he had come. From then on he became a beloved devotee of Baba. So much so that Baba personally used to stuff his plates and cups with food when he ate with Him.

10

Baba Saw Divinity in all Creatures

Baba never believed in long boring sermons. He made use of only day to day incidents to explain great philosophic truths. He convinced others that all creatures – cats, dogs, bulls, the destitute – have the same soul and deserve our love and pity like human beings.

DOG

One evening Laxmibai Shinde came to the Dwarkamai. On seeing her Baba said, " I am hungry." Laxmibai immediately went home, prepared food and came back and offered it to Baba hoping He would eat it but Baba to her surprise, picked up that food and gave it to a passing dog. "What is this, Baba? I ran home and cooked food with my own hands and You gave it to that dog without even eating a morsel. Why did You trouble me unnecessarily?" said Laxmibai. Then Baba said, "Why do you grieve without any reason? That dog too has a soul like human beings and though hunger is common, some can speak and some cannot but be sure, Laxmi, when one feeds the hungry, whether bird or beast one really feeds Me."

Mrs. Jog used to offer 'navaidya' to Baba and used to entreat Him to visit her lodging and have His meals there. Baba used to promise He would go but actually He never went to her place. One day while Mrs. Jog was preparing food, a stray dog went near her. Dogs, she thought, were unholy and polluting. She flung some burning wood at the dog. So it ran away. Then at noon when she took her 'navaidya' to Him and repeated her request to Baba to visit her house He said, "You are really wonderful, my dear lady. Daily you invite Me to come for meals to you but when I actually went to your house, you drove Me away by throwing burning wood to scare Me away."

One day Mhalsapati happened to hit a sickly looking village dog full of stinking sores. When he went to the Dwarkamai, Baba said to him, "Bhagat, there is a sickly dog like Me here in Shirdi and every one hits it." Then Baba showed the same marks on His body!

Kashinath Upasani stayed and cooked his own food in the Khandoba temple on Baba's orders He came to Baba every day to offer his 'navaidya' before he had his meals. One day, a black dog came and stood near him. It kept eyeing the food. But Upasani Baba did not give it anything to eat thinking that it was sacrilegious to offer food to a dog before it was offered to a deity. The dog followed him when he left for the Dwarkamai and then suddenly it disappeared from his sight. It was noon when he reached the Dwarkamai and offered his 'navaidya'. Baba asked him, "What for have you come here?" "To offer my 'navaidya' to you," said Upasani. "Why have you come all the way here in the scorching sun? I was there at Khandoba" said Baba. When Kashinath told Baba that there was only a dog there Baba said to him, " I was the dog. Since you refused Me food then, I am not going to touch it now."

Das Ganu says that once Nana Sahib Dengle offered Baba a plate full of various dainties. On seeing Dengle come with the plate. He suddenly shouted. Hearing His shouts, a black dog, passing through the lane ran up into the Dwarkamai and licked the food kept there by Dengle. Nana Sahib who witnessed this, was naturally shocked and looked at the dog with utter disgust. "Is it for this dog that I took all this trouble?" thought Dengle. Then Baba who is/was the soul of that dog, at once flung away the plate with its contents towards Nana and said to him, "Take away your plate. I won't touch it."

Mrs. Manager, a devotee from Mumbai, on a visit to Shirdi was busy cooking lunch when a dog turned up at the door. As the food was almost ready she fed the animal with unleavened bread and watched it gulp it down hurriedly. That afternoon when she went to the Dwarkamai Sai Baba thanked her for feeding Him. She expressed surprise as she had not met Baba earlier in the day. "The bread you fed Me was very delicious," Sai Baba explained to her and the others present, "I enjoyed it so much that it is still making Me belch. The dog, which came to your door is one with Me. I roam in many forms."

While another guru would have been content with a verbal discourse to see God in all creatures, Baba taught the same lesson by giving a practical demonstration.

Once, there was a strange sight in Shirdi. A small dog which was rabid was chasing bigger dogs and as the bigger dogs were afraid of its poisonous bite, they were running hither and thither. Seeing the chase some Shirdi folks took clubs in their hands and pursued the rabid dog with the intent to kill it. When all the dogs were running near the Mosque, the rabid dog ran up the steps of the Dwarkamai and sat behind Sai Baba behaving as if Baba alone were its sanctuary and only He could save it from death and that indeed proved to be true. The men dared not enter the Mosque with clubs in their hands but waited outside for the dog to step out of its safe hiding. Meanwhile, Baba vigorously abused and cursed them all for the heartless cruelty they wanted to inflict on that dog. When they told Him that the dog was rabid and must be killed He cursed them the more and asked them to get out from His sight. Then they warned Shamrao Jaykar and Dr. Pillay who were inside the Mosque with Baba that the dog was really mad and that they should be on their guard and went away from there. The small dog which ran to Baba bit neither Him nor His devotees but by morning it was cured of its madness by spending the night in the Dwarkamai.

CAT

One Hansraj of Bombay was a patient of chronic asthma. Baba advised him to avoid eating curd but curd was his favourite item in every meal. Of all the food items he relished curd the most. So, he could not follow Baba's instructions. He was prepared to give up his life rather than give up curd. As curd was not readily available in the Shirdi markets he gave standing orders to his wife to prepare it at home. Every day when they went for the morning 'arati' a cat would come and eat up the curd. This went on for two months. Hansraj lost his patience as he was deprived of his favourite food. One day he decided to miss the 'arati' to catch the thief red-handed. Then a cat came and Hansraj allowed it to enter, just to see how it reached the curd pot hung so high in a sling. In his presence the cat jumped up and devoured the curd. He allowed it to get down and when it was about to go away, he swung into action and gave it a beating with a cane. This is how he punished the thief in the very act of committing the theft. He was beside himself with joy for being successful. Later that day when the couple went to the Dwarkamai Baba said to Dixit, Booty, Jog, Shyama and others, "In Shirdi there is a lop-headed man who wants to die by eating sour and pungent things which I do not allow him to eat. Today, when I went to him as a cat, the fellow beat Me mercilessly on My back with a stick." Then Baba exposed His back by removing His 'kafani' and there were marks of beating.

BULL

Once a bull roamed about in the village gardens and fields and destroyed plants and crops. As it had become old and useless its master had stopped feeding it. So the inhabitants decided to send it to a cow pen where barren cows and old unwanted bulls were kept and fed on charity. They entrusted this work to Bhikoo Marwadi. Instead of taking the bull to the cow pen, he sold it to a butcher for fourteen rupees. To the people of Shirdi, he gave the impression that he had done the allotted duty. Omniscient Baba appeared Bayaji's dream and said, "You are enjoying sound sleep and you have placed Me in the hands of a butcher." Bayaji reported this to the village people. The search began. The bull was found at a butcher's place. It was brought back and Bhikoo Marwadi was put behind bars for two months.

BUFFALO

One day Baba told Mrs. Jog that one buffalo would come to her house that day and she should feed that animal with many 'pooran polis' and plenty of ghee. Taken aback, Mrs. Jog asked Baba to give her more particulars of that uncommon guest. He said the animal would come by itself and would appear at the southern door of her house. The lady had full faith in Baba's words and so she cooked the required number of 'polis'. Just then a buffalo appeared at the southern door. Mrs. Jog gladly placed all the 'polis' before the hungry animal. But to her great shock, soon after eating the dainty food, the animal collapsed and fell down at her door. Mrs. Jog thought that she had killed the animal and committed a sin and she would be troubled by the owner and by the police. She ran to Baba and told Him the facts and also expressed her doubts and fears which were soon allayed by Baba, "The buffalo had fulfilled all its desires in life except eating 'pooran polis' and when that desire was also fulfilled today, it passed from the animal form to another life. Don't worry. Go home now. You have helped her to get another life."

ANTS and FLIES

Once Baba asked Nana Sahib Chandorkar to prepare eight 'pooran polis' for His 'navaidya' and then go and take his meals. So Nana Sahib got 'polis' made and placed them before Baba when the 'arati' was over. A few flies and ants were attracted by them. They sat on the 'polis'. Baba even without touching them asked Nana to remove the 'prasad' from the Mosque but Nana insisted Baba should eat at least some 'polis'. Baba said that He had already eaten. "When did you eat, Baba? All the 'polis' are intact," said Nana. To which Baba said He had just eaten some of them. Nana Sahib was confused. He went away leaving the 'polis' in front of Baba. Then Baba sent for him and again asked him to take away the 'prasad' and have his meal, saying again that He had eaten Nana's 'navaidya' but Nana refused to obey His order. "Though you have been with Me for fourteen years, is this how much you have understood Me?" said Baba. Does Baba mean to you only this body, three and a half cubits high? Can't you see Me in the flies and ants that settled on the 'polis?" Then Baba lifted His hands and made some strange signs which revealed that Baba knew Nana's innermost soul and also the innermost soul of each and every living creature. Nana later removed the 'navaidya' plate. Then Baba said, "Nana, you must remember that I am in all the creatures."

CROW

Moreshwar Pradhan, during his first visit to Shirdi wanted to arrange a lunch in His honour and requested Baba to let him know who all were to be invited and what the menu was to be. 'Pooran poli' was to be the highlight of the meal. He told Pradhan, that Babu, Dada Kalekar's nephew must be invited. He assured Pradhan saying, "I will also come", even before Pradhan had made a formal request to Baba. The next day the lunch was prepared as directed by Baba and plates were served and Babu took his seat at one plate and another plate was served and set apart for Baba Himself. Then a crow came, sat on the plate and lifted a 'poli' off. All the guests who saw the incident were awfully delighted and felt that it was Baba who had come and kept His word.

THE LOW CASTE

Upasani Baba's 'navaidya' was rejected by Baba because he had not given food to a hungry dog. The next day he kept looking for the black dog but there was none. Instead, he found a low caste sickly-looking man leaning against the wall and looking at him preparing his food. Upasani Baba asked him to leave as it is improper for a low caste man to look on when a Brahmin is preparing his food. The next day when he reached the Dwarkamai Baba refused to accept his 'navaidya' as he had asked the sickly looking man to go away. Baba told Upasani Baba that He was the sickly looking man. Upasani Baba learnt the lesson that Baba is in every creature.

11

Baba's Command Over Elements

*B*aba had remarkable power to force events to happen according to His supreme will. He just commanded and His commands were obeyed.

Rain and Storm

On many occasions of storm or heavy rain, Baba just asked the clouds to go away and they glided away clearing the sky instantly.

M.W. Pradhan says, "On my first visit to Shirdi, there was a severe storm and rain for a quarter of an hour when I was with Baba at the Masjid. I thought if the rain continued a little longer like that the streams would swell. Then getting back to my home in Mumbai would be difficult, and Baba would not grant me early leave to go away. "Arey Allah! Ab bus kar. Mere bachey jane waley hain, unko sukh se jane de" (O God, enough of it. Stop the rain. My children have to return home. Let them go in comfort). As he spoke, the rain became gentler and feebler and I got the permission to leave."

One evening, a terrible storm threatened the village of Shirdi. Thunder and lightning were followed by a torrential downpour. The whole village was flooded, and anticipating disaster, people rushed to the Dwarkamai for help. Standing at the door of the Dwarkamai Sai Baba looked at the sky and shouted at the elements to stop their fury. Within minutes the rain subsided and all was calm.

Once when Dinkar Rao Jaykar, (son of Shyam Rao Jaykar, the artist who painted Baba's portrait when Baba was alive), was in the

Masjid with Baba, a severe storm started howling. The wind and the rain were fierce. After a few minutes, Sai Baba stepped on the edge of the premises and cried out to the storm, 'Stop a bit.' And the storm abated very quickly.

Fire

Once, the fire in the dhuni at the Dwarkamai started burning very brightly. The flames rose so high that they were about to touch the rafters. Everyone in the Dwarkamai feared that the roof would get burnt. But Baba rapped the pillars with his sataka, and with every stroke, the flames came down till they reached a safe level.

On another occasion when hay stocked in Shirdi fields caught fire, the crops were in danger of being burnt. Baba went there and drew a circle of water around the burning hay, stating that fire would not spread beyond that line. The farmers found that Baba's control of fire was unique, for the fire stopped as soon as the stock marked by Baba was burnt down.

Everyone knows that He produced fire for Chand Patil's chillum.

Water

When Ramnaumi festival was to start, there was a water problem in Shirdi. Baba solved this problem by throwing some flowers into the wells. Immediately the dry well was overflowing with water and the brackish water of the other well became sweet.

Moreover Baba produced water for Chand Patil's chillum also.

Roof

Once when Baba and his devotees were having lunch, a portion of the dilapidated Mosque started crumbling with a loud noise. Baba lifted his hand and said loudly, 'Wait! Wait!' The noise stopped. When after finishing the meal everyone came out, a big portion of the mosque came down with a shattering noise exactly at the spot where Baba and the others were sitting.

Snake Bite
Not only rain and fire, even snakes had to obey Baba. During Baba's time Shirdi was infested with snakes. One of its victim was Shama, Baba's close devotee. Baba stopped the spread of poison by a command to the serpent and by keeping Shama awake the whole night, chewing neem leaves.

Scorpion-Bite
Once Bapu Sahib Jog became a victim of a scorpion-bite and he complained to Baba. Baba said, "Go. The pain will go soon." And it did go soon.

12

Male Child by Baba's Grace

According to the Hindu scriptures a son is a son and a daughter simply a daughter and isn't the same as a son or equal to a son. A sonless man has no salvation and that was the reason which brought Nana Sahib Dengle and Gopal Rao Gund to Shirdi. This desire motivated scores of others to seek Baba's grace. Baba conferred progeny for the mere asking, when the seeker came to Him with love, affection and faith. At times He gave His blessings without any expressed prayers. Some times He brought the deceased after several years, back into the womb of his loving mother. Some times, He transferred the soul which He loved, to the womb of another devotee of His. At times He gave some fruit to the parents and at times a coconut was given and at times a simple word of His was enough to bestow an issue on the most hopeless case.

There is a long list of devotees who went to Baba to get the curse of being sonless removed. At Neemgaon, Nana Sahib Dengle had two wives but no son. Baba blessed him with a son and henceforth people started flocking to Him for His blessings for a son.

Damodar Rasane of Ahmadnagar had two wives but no issue. He consulted astrologers who after consulting his horoscope told him that he had no prospects of having an issue since Ketu had occupied an adverse place among the stars and planets controlling his life. So learning of Baba and His wonderful miracles, he thought of trying his luck with Baba.

About the year 1900, one Rege sent Baba mangoes from Goa. He distributed the luscious mangoes among the devotees and kept aside four mangoes. In the Mosque, there were people who had their eyes on those delicious mangoes. But Baba said that those mangoes were for Damia. People argued that Damia was not in the Masjid neither was he in Shirdi. Baba said that he had arrived in Shirdi and would be there in the Masjid soon. When he arrived Baba gave him those mangoes for his younger wife. With that they had not one or two but eight children! Infertility was cured with mangoes.

Gopal Rao Gund was a Circle Inspector at Kopergaon. He married thrice but had no issue. He heard of Sai Baba, sought His blessings and later had a son. It was in gratitude for His blessings that Gopal Rao thought of celebrating the annual 'urs' in honour of Sai Baba.

Hari Vinayak Sathe had only daughters when his wife expired. He was already fifty-five when he got ready for a second marriage after Baba assured him that he would get a son and he did get a son.

Hans Raj of Sakori was a devotee of Sai Baba and Narsingh Maharaj. He was suffering from asthma and he also had no issue even years after his marriage. When he approached Narsingh Maharaj for blessings, the latter told him that his body was possessed by a spirit which was preventing the birth of children. He advised him to go to Sai Baba of Shirdi who would give him two slaps and thereby exorcise the spirit. Accordingly the couple visited Baba in 1916. When they bowed to Baba in the Mosque, Baba slapped Hans Raj twice and said, "Evil spirit go away! Later the couple was blessed with an offspring.

Mr. Pillay and Sushilamma had been married for several years but had no child and their relatives were pressing Mr. Pillay to marry a second time to get an issue. One day in 1952, Sushilamma's brother gave her a picture of Baba and asked her to worship Him and said that Baba might bless her with an offspring. She started

Male Child by Baba's Grace

worshipping Him and in 1954, she was blessed with a son, whom they named after Baba.

In 1957, the Bhatnagar couple was blessed with a son due to Sai Baba's grace. They had come to Baba after trying many doctors and worshipping many gods and goddesses.

Mrs. Chandrabai Borkar was a Sai devotee since 1898. In 1918 when Baba took 'Samadhi' she was 48 years old. Before His 'Samadhi' Baba, once asked what her desire was. She said that she need not mention it as Baba knew it. She yearned for a male child even at that age but had not conceived even once. The people and the doctors around her pooh – poohed her desire as conception at that age was unthinkable. In 1921 her menses stopped. The doctors examined her and diagnosed a tumour and recommended an operation. Her faith in Baba was so much that she decided to wait for ten months and then go in for the operation. In her 51st year she gave birth to a son! At the time of her delivery she had neither the services of a doctor nor of a nurse nor any medicine.

Septnaker was a pleader practicing in Akkalkot. In 1913 he lost his only son. After this he lost his peace of mind. He went on a pilgrimage but it was of no use. Ultimately he went to Shirdi Sai Baba, who promised to bring that very child back in his wife's womb and He fulfilled His promise.

A lady of Pune was issueless. She believed that if she got a coconut from Baba she would bear a child. Whenever she started for Shirdi some obstacle or the other cropped up. One night, Baba appeared in her dream and gave her a coconut. The next morning when she woke up, she actually found one coconut on her bed! She was amazed at Baba's 'leela' and vowed that she would offer one coconut at Shirdi if she were blessed with a son and she got the opportunity to go to Shirdi and fulfill her promise.

Rustamji Shahpuri Wadia was a wealthy mill owner of Nanded. He was unhappy because he was issueless. Das Ganu advised him to seek Baba's blessings. The couple went to Shirdi and offered gifts and 'dakshina' and in the course of time Rustamji had as many as twelve issues of whom four survived.

Mrs. Sukhram Aurangabadkar of Sholapur had been married for 27 years but despite innumerable visits and vows to various gods and goddesses, she had remained chidless. As a last resort, she went to Shirdi and stayed there for two months to get an opportunity to talk to Baba in private. Shyama had to intervene to broach the topic. Within twelve months of her visit she was the proud mother of a son.

One Shinde from Harda had seven daughters but no son. He went to Gangapur in 1903, prayed to Lord Datta that should a son be born to him within a year he would take the child to Gangapur and have Datta's 'darshan'. Shinde had a son within a year but failed to fulfil his vow. And then in 1911 he came to Shirdi. Baba said to him, "You are very much conceited. Where was a son in your destiny? I tore My body and gave you one" and thus Baba showed Shinde that he was blessed even before he had heard of Him or addressed any prayer to Him.

The few children who were born to Santaram Nachane died in their infancy. In 1915 he went to Baba as his mother-in-law was very anxious to obtain Baba's blessings for a son for him. At her request Shyama took Nachane's wife to Baba in the Mosque and asked her to offer a coconut to Baba. When that was done, Baba threw the coconut into Mrs. Nachane's 'pallav' and as he did this tears were brimming in Baba's eyes. Nachane did have a son but he did not live long.

Laxman Munge had children but all died in their infancy. So in 1903 Munge went to Shirdi and wept before Baba and prayed that he be given one son with a longer life. Then Baba said to him, "Why do you ask for one? I will give you two." After that Munge had two sons and two daughters and they lived the normal length of life and died of old age.

Mhalsapati, was the Khandoba priest, but when Baba came to Shirdi, he dedicated himself to His service. He began to live and move and sleep in His company. He developed detachment in life and never cared to continue his family life by living with his wife. He had one daughter who was married and had moved to her husband's house. His only son was dead. One day Baba said to him, "Bhagat, look here. Listen to My words. Each day you come and sleep here and not with your wife and you have only a daughter living. Daughters are like a tamarind fruit but a son is like a mango. Go and sleep in your house and you will soon get a son." Baba said these words in 1896 on Janamashtami day. But in spite of this express direction Mhalsapati refused to go and it was Kashiram who forcibly dragged him and locked him in his house. Then he started living in his own house along with his wife and had a son within a year on the next Janamashtami day.

Not only human beings even animals were blessed with young ones by Baba's grace. Kasim's mare had not produced a foal for a long time. So, he decided to give the first born to Baba if she foaled. The result was Shyamkaran, Baba's pet.

13

Baba as Protector/Saviour

*D*iverse were the ways in which Baba saved His men and their kith and kin, whether far or near, from disease, disaster and death by giving them timely help as well as necessary protection. Some times he warned them in person of the coming dangers and some times by means of a dream, some times in answer to a devotee's prayer and some times even without such a prayer to Him. All this showed that He was really an all – pervasive, divine power.

Once, an astrologer told Booty Sahib that that day was very inauspicious for him as it could end in his death. When Baba came to know this He said, "I will see how death kills you. You don't fear." That day when Booty Sahib went to answer the call of nature a snake did appear and it could have killed him but because of Baba's assurance the snake could do no harm to Mr. Booty Sahib.

Once Bala Sahib Mirikar, the Mamlatdar of Kopergaon, was on the way to Chittali village on some official visit. He halted at Shirdi. When he was sitting in the Dwarkamai, Baba suddenly asked him, "Do you know our Dwarkamai?" Mirikar did not reply as he did not know what Baba wanted to convey. Then Baba pointing to His Mosque continued to explain, " This Masjidmai confers happiness on all those who seek her shelter. She is kind and merciful and ensures safety from all the dangers if they lie in her motherly lap under her protective wings." Thus, detailing the nature and virtues of His Mosque , He gave Mirikar the 'udhi' but before he left, Baba again asked him if he knew the long Bava, a serpent, gesticulating with His left fist and imitating a hooded serpent He said, "The killer can do nothing when there is saviour. He asked

Shyama to accompany Mirikar to Chittali and then return after enjoying some fun there. Very unwillingly Mirikar took Shyama with him to Chittali where a surprise and a shock of his life was waiting for him. When he was lying down in the Maruti temple there reading an old newspaper to pass time, in the light of the lamp, a serpent was noticed quietly resting near Mirikar's waist. Shyama and others brought sticks and managed to kill the reptile before it could do any harm to the Kopergaon visitor. Mirikar and Shyama understood how Baba had warned them of the lurking danger.

Mrs. Manager was at Shirdi. It was a dark night. There was no light where she was walking about. But suddenly and abruptly she stopped. There was no reason to account for her stopping. For some unknown reason she felt she must stop and after some time a light was brought to the very place where she would have put her foot at the next step. There was a serpent lying quietly. Of course, if she had put her foot, the consequences might have been serious, if not fatal. The light showed what danger she had escaped. Why and how she stopped so abruptly and how the light came at so opportune a moment to show her the danger, was a mystery. The only answer is, the all seeing and ever watchful and protective eyes of Sai Baba were on her.

In 1947, there was no electricity in most of the villages of India. A girl named Indira was reading a religious book by the light of a lamp. It was 8 o'clock. A 'pujari' came with a plate of 'Prasadam'. She had to leave her bed to receive it. When she came back she found a snake on the bed. At the appropriate time Baba had made her leave her bed, which saved her from the mishap.

Once Mukand Lele Shastri went with Chandorkar in a tonga. On the way the horse reared and the carriage overturned. But both of them came off without any hurt. Baba was at that time at Shirdi. He sounded a 'shankh' and said, "Nana is about to die. But I will not let him die." Eight days later both of them went to Shirdi. Then Bapu Sahib Jog told Lele what Baba had said eight days back and asked him if that was true. Lele confirmed it and narrated the whole incident.

Sitting in front of the 'dhuni' Baba all of a sudden thrust His hand into the fire and got his hand burnt. When asked why He had behaved in that manner Baba narrated that a black-smith's wife was blowing the bellows with a child on her lap. Unnoticed, the child had slipped into the furnace. Baba had thrust His hand to take out the child from the fire. What if He hurt His hand in the process!

Baba saved Dixit's eight year old daughter Vatsali when an almirah fell on her and she escaped without any injury.

Bapurao Purwarkar had lost his parents when he was an infant. As it usually happens his property was usurped by his relatives. He went to Shirdi on foot with only three annas in his pocket. But he earned lakhs of rupees through Sai Baba's grace. As he had a maternal uncle there, he looked after his fields. Under his supervision, the fields had bumper crops. Then, he got a chance to look after a neighbour's fields also. A day came when he got his own bungalow built with fruit trees. As per Swami Sharan Anand the bungalow can still be seen on the way to Rahata.

Baba saved Atma Ram Sawant, a police inspector, from death in the year 1929 during Hindu-Muslim riots in Bombay. Sawant had a high fever and a severe headache. A European officer on his round of duty, on seeing that Sawant was really ill, relieved him saying that he would inform the Superintendent of this. Unluckily, an hour after Sawant was relieved, the riot reached its highest pitch and the officer was killed in it. Baba had inspired the European officer to relieve Samant from duty. Probably death would have taken Atma Ram and not the officer.

In 1916, while Shyamrao Jaykar, the illustrious painter was living in a suburb of Bombay, thieves broke into his house. It was about 2 a.m. when they succeeded in pulling out some iron bars fixed in a window of the room where Baba's photograph was kept and worshipped. They would have easily entered the house and ransacked and robbed. But a barber was sleeping in a different part of the house. It was his habit to get up daily at four in the morning and then go round the house to answer the call of nature. But on that night he got up at two and went round the house as usual before the thieves had effected entry into Jaykar's room. They saw the barber and started running. On seeing them run he shouted, "Thieves! Thieves!" and every one got up and chased away the fleeing miscreants. Jaykar later found that they were awakened just in time to prevent the thieves from entering into his room of worship and all believed that it was Baba who came in the barber's form and successfully averted a major calamity that was to befall the painter.

In 1917, Shyamrao Jaykar was living in Pune. His house was old and dilapidated. Its walls and ceilings were all crumbling. To prevent the dust falling from above he had strung up a cloth under the ceiling. One night, in the room, where Baba's picture was kept with a burning lamp, the ceiling cloth fell down with a thud since some loose bricks of the ceiling had fallen on it. So the debris descended on the floor along with the cloth. As the ceiling cloth covered the entire ceiling it was natural for the cloth with the bricks to fall on the child and the lamp. But He who was present there in the form of His photo, willed otherwise. So, both the debris and the cloth fell within a foot of the lamp and the child and did not touch either of them. If they had fallen on the child he would have been crushed to death and if they had fallen on the lamp, fire would have killed the child and set Jaykar's room ablaze.

Nagesh Atma Ram Samant says that years back there was a scorpion in his cap. He did not notice it and put it on at Shirdi and he took it off at Bombay some 12 hours later. As he was going to place it on the peg, he saw a scorpion inside it. It had not hurt him all the time he had worn the cap.

Some time in 1913 when Shantaram Nachane was at Shirdi, Baba said in his presence, "We should not trust mad men" and the remark being such a common truism, it did not strike Nachane as being addressed to him, warning him of the coming danger. What happened in 1914 showed him that Baba had so kindly given him an early warning. In 1914, Nachane was working as Treasure Master at Dahanu town. One day when he was doing his 'pooja' at home, worshipping the photograph of Baba and other deities one Rambhau Phanse who was deranged, was standing near the door of his 'pooja' room. Since he was considered to be a harmless creature, no one minded him. Then suddenly, when Nachane was deeply engrossed in 'pooja' Phanse pounced upon him, grabbed his neck with both his hands and began to bite his throat saying, "I will drink your blood." Nachane at once thrust his 'pooja' spoon and his fingers into the madman's mouth and with his other hand tried to free his throat from the grip of the murderous hands. Nachane's mother, too, rushed to help him and Phanse, loosened his grip. As Phanse's nails had dug deep into the throat and he was nearly strangled to death, Nachane was unconscious for quite some time but after medical treatment he regained his senses. After this incident, when Shantaram Nachane went to Shirdi, Baba pointed to Nachane and told Anna Chinchinikar, " Anna, if I had delayed even by an instant this man was finished. The mad man had seized his throat with his hands and I ran and helped extricate him. What is to be done? If I do not save my children then who will save them?"

On 31-3-1915 Balwant Nachane, had a thrilling experience. At that time he was travelling with Phanse and other friends in a bullock-cart in the dense forests of Ranikhet pass which was known to be infested with tigers. The night was dark and suddenly the bulls yoked to the cart took fright and stopped moving. They started moving backwards. Luckily their cart was not at the edge of the road otherwise in that steep and narrow pass, if the cart had swerved a little they would have fallen into the ravine and instantly met their death. Then, Phanse pointed out to Nachane what exactly the trouble was in front of their cart. On the road sat a tiger. Phanse wished to get down from the cart and place a stone or log beside the wheels to prevent it from falling into the ravine and asked Nachane, in the meanwhile to hold the reins. Nachane held the reins and suddenly started crying aloud, " Hail Sai Baba. Run Sai Baba" and his friends also joined him in the appeal and the tiger got frightened by the cries and passing by their cart, it disappeared in the darkness.

Baba as Protector/Saviour

There was a break – in and robbery in the locality where Ramchander Dev, a devotee of Baba lived in Bombay. When he saw the inmates of the house who had been beaten severely by the robbers and had sustained grievous injuries, he got terribly frightened and prayed to Baba to come to his aid and protect his family. That very night, Baba appeared in his dream and said that He would come with ten Pathans and that he need not worry. About that time, the washermen, who did their washing on railway property, were refused permission to continue in that area. So, ten of them went to Ramchander Dev and offered to build their own huts there in his lane. Dev readily agreed and felt safe and secure.

In 1916, Ramchander Modak was laid up with chronic cough and fever. A doctor friend of his attended on him and prescribed chloral hydrate for the bronchitis as that was his diagnosis of the ailment he was suffering from. Mrs. Modak, however, had a suspicion that the case was not so simple. So, praying to Baba she sent for Dr. Buckley. When he came and examined Modak he saw the bottle of chloral hydrate lying there. He took the earlier doctor, his subordinate, to task for his wrong diagnosis and declared the case to be of double pneumonia. He threw away that bottle as it was extremely harmful for Modak. Then, by Dr. Buckley's treatment and Baba's grace, Modak recovered health. He was convinced it was really Baba's grace that inspired his wife to send for an experienced doctor before that deadly medicine was given to him.

One day in March 1911 in the forenoon, Baba said he had intense pain in His belly and asked His men to fetch a turban. When that was done, Baba wound it around His body and asked two men to hold its ends on either side and pull it on each side, which was done for quite some time. The men were shocked at Baba's unusual conduct. After some time, He told them to stop pulling and said, " I have relief now" No one knew relief from what but a little later they came to know that a lady devotee of His at Neemgaon had safely delivered a child after a long and difficult labour. Then it was clear that Baba's actions were to save her.

Ramchander Samant, during his convalescence was in his house at Amala. In February, 1915, he got a sudden fit while trying to get up from his bed His wife and others were much frightened since they thought that the fall might result in death. At that time Ramchander had a vision in which he saw some 8 or 10 darkish beings with sticks and spears, dressed in the manner of 'Yamdooths' or messengers of death had surrounded him and he said to himself. "What is all this? Why are they beating me?" He did not feel any pain but still he had the feeling that he was being beaten and assaulted and simultaneously there was a light. Ramchander saw a hand moving and sweeping aside those horrible creatures. He also saw a portion of a white 'kafani' below that hand. Then he woke up to full consciousness and sat up. Samant had not sustained any injury from his fall. The only damage was to his spectacles, which were broken. At that time Samant had no faith in Baba's help, but his relatives, had no doubt whatsoever of Baba's help.

Gopal Narain Ambedakar of Pune had served a decade in the Excise department and retired from service. He was without any employment and his efforts to secure a job all proved in vain. His financial condition, therefore grew from bad to worse. For seven years he lived in this state of joblessness though each year he visited Shirdi and told Baba about his state. At last in 1916, when he could no longer bear the plight he came to Shirdi with his wife and stayed there for full two months and finding no way out nor any ray of hope, one night he brooded over his condition and decided to end his life of utter misery. When this idea entered his head, and he was about to go and jump into a nearby well, Sagun Meru Naik who was running a boarding house near the Ambedekars' quarters, turned up and said to Gopal, "Did you ever read about the life of Akkalkot Maharaj?" and unasked handed him a book on that Maharaj. Ambedekar took that book in his hands and casually opened a page, he found a story that showed how that Maharaj by his timely appearance, saved his devotee from committing suicide by jumping into a well. He advised him to bear the fruits of his previous lives with courage and fortitude and not to end his precious life. On reading this story, Gopal thought it was Baba who had given him that advice and prevented him from ending his life. Then, he got Baba's blessings and came back home and studied astrology, became well-known and later, lived a happy life.

There is an instance of Baba saving Smt. Sushilamma from a serious scandal. Her teenaged nephew (sister's son) was staying with her. He wanted his marriage to be performed and the elders scolded him for his haste. The boy then swallowed rat poison and was in a critical condition. The doctors gave up hope of his survival. Every one including her sister said that Smt. Sushilamma might have poisoned him because of some grudge against him. So, she prayed to Baba to save his life so that he might reveal the truth and save her from the scandal. He did survive most miraculously and he confessed what he had done and Smt. Sushilamma's innocence was thus proved. Otherwise the scandal would have been a life–long torture for her.

Mr. Gopalareddy says, "Our baby was being brought home from the maternity hospital on the 14th day of her birth. I was handing over the baby from the platform to my wife who had boarded the train. Unfortunately the baby slipped from my hands and fell down between the platform and the train. She did not cry and we could not make out whether she was badly hurt. The baby was disabled. Her hands and legs became useless. The doctors tried their best but could only save her life. The disabled limbs did not grow well and remained thin. She could not walk and she dragged her legs along as she moved on her buttocks. Even at the age of four, the girl could not speak. We were heart-broken at her plight but were helpless. Luckily Sh. E Bhardwaj visited our house. We put the sad plight of our four-year-old daughter before him. He glanced at her benignly, passed his hands over her limbs and said that by Baba's grace the child would recover soon. He then gave the girl 'Prasadam'; which he had offered to Baba's picture. To our surprise, the girl started walking from the next day and now she can run and climb the staircase. She has gained her speech. She sings Baba's 'bhajans'.

A gentleman who was in Udaipur, was suffering from a stomach ulcer. His wife was anxious about him at Kamgaon. One night she had a terrible dream. She saw her husband's body being carried to the cremation ground and she was telling her brother that she preferred death to widowhood. A strange faqir with a radiant face said to her, "Why do you weep? Your husband will soon come to life." Later she came to know that on the same day her husband's condition had grown hopeless but then he soon recovered quite mysteriously. She later saw a picture of Baba and recognized Him as the Faqir who had come in her dream and she started worshipping Him ignoring the criticism and objections of her co-religionists. After some time, they visited Shirdi and she recognized the place where the Faqir stood in her dream. It was the Dwarkamai.

Champaklal Manakwala of Ahamdabad was laid up with dropsy and intestinal ulcer from 1948-1952. He found it difficult even to drink water. His weight had increased to 300 pounds and he used to spit blood on account of the ulcer. The doctors who examined him in 1952 declared that he was sure to pass away in one or two days' time. In a mood of utter helplessness, he started worshipping the picture of Baba that his friends had given him. Then, another friend gave him two books on Baba in Gujrati. Those, too he started reading. A few days later the doctors examined him and decided that he had only two hours more to live! As soon as they left the room a mysterious light appeared in front of Champaklal Manakwala. Behind it appeared Sai Baba. It was about 1p.m. Baba said, "Son, don't be afraid. I have taken away all your sufferings." The wonder of it is that even his mother could see Baba. He, then told them to send Mankwala's son to Shirdi and walked out of the room. Champaklal Manakwala was worried whether his son could travel alone to Shirdi safely and in case he died, his son's presence and would be necessary to perform his last rites. At last he decided to abide by Baba's words and sent his son to Shirdi. At about 6 p.m,

Baba again appeared to him and said, "Don't be afraid. I am with your son. You will receive a telegram that he has reached Shirdi safely by 12 noon tomorrow."

A few minutes later the doctors again examined the patient and thought that he was dying. They mocked at his accounts of Baba's assurance. Indeed, nothing happened to Champaklal Manakwala and the next day they received a telegram from Shirdi regarding his son's safe arrival there. For 24 hours precisely from the moment of the receipt of the telegram, Champaklal Manakwala passed excess of urine and suffered a severe attack of diarrhoea. Soon his body weight came down to 75 pounds. His pulse and heart beat were normal. The doctors agreed that his recovery was indeed a miracle of Sai Baba. Within the next two months Champaklal Manakwala regained his normal health.

14

Baba as Helper

Baba is Baba. There can be no comparison with any one else. He was always helping His devotees as long as He was in flesh and blood and is helping them even now. The instances are too numerous to relate.

Laxman Govind Munge wanted to get married but had no money. He went to Rahata to ask his uncle for financial help. There he met Baba for the first time. On being asked, he told Baba the purpose of his visit. Baba, a Faqir promised to give him one to two thousand rupees but asked him to go back to Nasik and not to worry. At Nasik, a money lender lent him money for the marriage and by Baba's grace he was able to solemnize the marriage.

Abdul Dalali's son was to be married and Abdul prayed for Baba's permission. But each time Baba was asked for His permission, He put it off and whenever he wrote to Baba for leave the usual reply sent back by Baba was 'Allah Malik hai'. At last after three years, Baba wrote that the marriage may be solemenised and He Himself fixed the date for the marriage and ordered him to celebrate the marriage on that particular day. Dalali was poor and he wondered how a man like him could make the provision of funds required for the wedding. He had agreed to pay the expenses of the bride's party. And much worried, he looked to Baba and prayed for aid. The aid was soon provided by Baba in a wonderful way. Some ten days prior to the wedding, he was entrusted with an unexpected contract and an unexpected advance. Thus, he got some relief and with similar, unexpected help from some other sources, Dalali was able to celebrate the wedding on the exact date and time fixed in advance by Baba in Shirdi.

A cashier of a well-known Mumbai firm ran away with a large sum and came to Shirdi to save himself. The work of searching for the culprit was entrusted to the firm's manager, a Sai devotee. He tried his utmost to trace the culprit but to no avail. He was on the verge of abandoning the search when he decided to seek Baba's advice. To his surprise the culprit was there shampooing Baba's legs. The culprit got nervous and sought Baba's forgiveness. Baba advised him to confess his fault before his employer and seek his forgiveness. The culprit followed Baba's instructions to the letter and was exempted from criminal proceedings. On the other hand, the manager also got appreciation for handling the case so dexterously.

Sh. H. V. Sathe wanted to see the land purchased by his father-in-law. His father-in-law refused to accompany him. Then, he expected his wife to accompany him. She, too, refused to go with him because of the reason given by her father. Sathe got so furious that he took up a whip and was about to whip her when Megha rushed in saying., " Sahibji, Sahibji. You are wanted by Baba immediately." Sathe had to suspend the heinous action. When he went before Baba the omniscient Baba said to him, "Where is the hurry to see the land? It is there." Sathe hung his head in shame and thanked Baba for stopping him from perpetuating cruelty on his wife. His wife, too, thanked Baba for saving her from being whipped. By His timely intervention Baba helped both of them.

In 1915, Tarkhand was jobless after he gave up the mill manager's post. During that period he came to Shirdi with his wife. The couple spent a few days there. When Mr. Tarkhand went to seek permission to leave Baba asked them to go via Pune rather than via Manmad. This was a longer route. Due to financial constraints, the wife resented this but the husband adhered to Baba's instructions. At Pune, they spent some time with a local friend. There Mr. Tarkhand came to know through his friend that a job was available in a mill. He was immediately introduced to the mill owner and instantly he was employed. There was no need to pray or tell Baba anything. Baba was well aware of His devotee's interests.

Mr. Tarsem Kapoor of Ghaziabad was coming to Delhi to catch a train to Shirdi. On the way Mr. Kapoor and his family got stuck in a traffic jam and knew for certain that they would not be able to catch the train. To their surprise the train was late. Baba had come to Mr. Kapoor's help.

It was November 1937. Narsimha Swami was to travel from Tiruannamalai to Chennai, a distance of 140 miles by train. A friend, Mr. Tulsidas Sahni, offered to take them (Swamiji and Radha Krishnaji) by car saying that they would pass time singing together. Swamiji agreed. On the way the car came to a halt. It was raining incessantly and there was no possibility of getting the car repaired in that desolate place. They kept sitting in the car for 45 minutes. In the mean while a car came from Tiruannamalai. It was going to Chennai. The driver was the sole occupant of the car. He offered to give them a lift. When they sat in the car, the driver told them that he could not explain the day's events as he had written to his family that he was extending his visit by four days. But at 11am he had impulsively started for Chennai. Now, he realized the reason when he saw them stranded in that helpless condition. Sai Baba had intervened because of Sh. Narsimha Swamiji.

In 1942, during World War II Dr. R. Govind Rao M.B.B.S; M.S. (Yale) was posted at Anantpur. His search for a residence led him to the house of Mr. Ramaswami whose six year old daughter had met with an accident. Ten days earlier her clothes had caught fire. Her body was full of foul smelling pus and the hospital had discharged her thinking that no human help could save her. For six days she had been unconscious. So, the parents were crying when the doctor reached there. The moment Dr. Rao was introduced to Ramaswami, the later remarked that Baba had sent medical aid. The doctor was surprised as he had never heard of Sai Baba. He knew for certain that it was an hopeless case, still as a doctor he took up the job. He covered his nose with a piece of cloth and started cleaning the wounds. He removed about 180 maggots and it took him nearly three hours. During the whole process the girl did not respond. He administered whatever medicine he could. At night, the girl's parents applied 'udhi' on her forehead. The next day, when the doctor came to see the patient, she had improved miraculously. She could talk to the doctor, a miracle that he had never seen before. It took him six months to cure her fully.

Bhikaji Mahadev Bidwa was a peon in Sai Sansthan at a meagre salary of Rs. 36 p.m. His sister was sick and he wanted to show her to a good doctor. But with his meagre salary he could not afford it. He knew for certain that Baba would not let him down. His faith bore fruit. On 5-12-1951 there came a doctor, a devotee, who treated Bidwa's sister.

There was an All India Devotees' Convention. Narsimha Swami and Sh. Radha Krishna Swami were to attend it. When they boarded the train at Chennai, Swamiji realized that they had left certain important papers at their host's residence. Swamiji asked Radha Krishnaji to go back to the host's place to collect those papers. The train was scheduled to leave at 9:30. The second bell rang when Radha Krishnaji alighted and proceeded to the host's house. It was a 10 to 15 minutes walk. In the meanwhile, the guard blew the whistle and showed the green flag. The driver wanted to start the train but it would not move even an inch. When it was examined, there was nothing wrong with the brake system. Exactly at 10 p.m. Radha Krishnaji arrived with the papers. In the meanwhile, a crowd had gathered near Swamiji. The station staff and the driver perceiving the crowd, suspected some mishap and came over to Swamiji's compartment. Narsimha Swamiji told the driver of the train, "Now you go and start the train. It will start. There will be no difficulty." The driver then went and started the train, and it moved smoothly.

Rao Bahadur Dhumal was an honorary president of the Nasik District Local Board. He had to personally sign thousands of papers without the use of facsimile seal, a procedure which took many hours each day. A peon had to carry these papers to him and blot each signature and after some hours the work was over and the papers were sent back to the office. One day, when the papers were before him, a visitor came and stayed talking with him till midnight and so the signatures had to be postponed till the next day. The next morning, he found no time and sent back the papers to the office. When he returned that night, he found only that day's papers brought to him for his signatures. When he wanted the previous day's papers, he found that they all bore his signatures! How thousands of signatures had been affixed to the papers he could not guess. He had no other explanation for it except Sai Baba and His superhuman powers had done it.

Babu Tendulkar, the son of Raghunath Tendulkar of Mumbai, was due to appear for a medical examination but some astrologers who were consulted told him that since his stars were not favourable, he would not be able to pass the exam. Later Savitribai, his mother, personally went to Shirdi and explained her son's problem and the astrologers' reading to Baba. Baba advised her to ask her son to keep faith in Him and to disregard the prediction of the astrologers and palmists and appear for the examination with courage. Told of Baba's blessings, the boy studied hard and boldly appeared for the medical examination. He did well in the written papers but he did not wish to appear for oral tests. He was sure that he would not be able to get pass marks in the written examination. But quite unexpectedly the examiner who knew the boy, sent word to him that he had passed his written tests and so he faced the oral tests boldly and later was declared to have passed in both the oral and written tests in the examination.

The son of a gentleman from Thane ran away from his house and though the father searched for him in many places for several days there was no hope of finding the boy. So, the father went to Shirdi and told his story to Sai Baba. Baba said, "Well, you may go . You will meet your son on your way back to your home." The man felt happy. He was standing on the platform after getting down from the train and there he saw his son getting down from a Mumbai local!

Baba as Helper

Due to party factions in a certain village, a man was falsely implicated in a case and out of fear, absconded from that place and came to Shirdi with eight hundred rupees in cash and two costly gold rings. He stayed in the Dixitwada and ate in the eatery of Sagunmeru Naik. Every day he used to go to the Mosque for Baba's 'darshan' and Baba never talked to him. Then, one day Baba asked for a 'dakshina' of eight hundred rupees from that man. He readily and gladly gave it to Baba. Slowly He took away all his money as His 'dakshina' then at his request Sagunmeru Naik wrote to his brother and asked him to bring some money to Shirdi. After that His brother came to Shirdi with a thousand rupees and immediately left Shirdi after giving him the money. Baba gradually took that amount also as 'dakshina' and so that man was reduced literally to a penniless state. Then the Nizam's Police came to Shirdi in search of that man and when he sighted the police, the man straight away went to the Mosque and took refuge there. The Police searched for him at every place in Shirdi including Baba's Mosque but though he was there, he was not seen and so the police gave up their search and went away empty-handed from Shirdi. When the man learnt of their departure, he got up and bowed to Baba who blessed him and asked him to take his meals the next day in the wada and go back home fearlessly as his troubles had come to an end. The next day, even before he left Shirdi, he got a letter from his brother saying that he had been acquitted of the charge and had also been awarded damages many times more than the amount he had earlier given as His 'dakshina'.

Once during the Dusehra festival of 1915 He said to Kaka Dixit, "Kaka, the good and the bad both come here. We should see and regard them both impartially. Isn't it?". Kaka Dixit could not understand the importance of these words. Soon there came a clerk who bowed to Baba. There was a warrant of arrest against him for having misappropriated his master's money and he had run to Baba to save his skin. Strangely, the officer of that clerk was also present with Baba when he came. Baba as usual, told a story of embezzlement of money and the pending arrest warrants concealing the name of the man involved. Then, Baba asked the clerk to go away from the Mosque and have his meal. He told his senior to remain with Him. When the clerk had gone for his meals Baba had a private talk with him. The senior officer was worried that he would be accused of not doing his duty well, if he let the dishonest clerk escape. Soon the clerk returned, and following Baba's advice, he surrendered in the court. He pleaded guilty and as the complainant did not press for a severe sentence, he was given a nominal sentence. The senior officer was sent back by Baba and by Baba's grace, no one blamed him for any lapse on his part.

15

Baba as Ashutosh

A god who fulfills your wishes instantly is Ashutosh. Many episodes prove that Baba deserves this epithet and is aptly called Ashutosh.

One day in 1911 Balwant Khojokar of Thane took leave of Baba. When he had walked a considerable distance, he had a strong desire to see Baba once more. But once a devotee took leave, he was not supposed to return. Just as these ideas passed through his mind he glanced at the Lendi Bagh and there, peeping through the hedge, was Baba's face. He said, "Are you going? Well, go."

One Gadge Patel was transferred to a far off place. He was sad that he could not visit Shirdi and get Baba's 'udhi' and blessings. In this state of mind he boarded the train. The next moment he was surprised to find a small packet of 'udhi' on the windowsill of the compartment. When he visited Shirdi later, Baba said to the other devotees that though Gadge Patel could not visit him earlier, He had sent him 'udhi'.

Captain Hate wanted to keep in the pooja room a rupee sanctified by Baba. He sent one rupee through his friend Sawant Ram. When Sawant Ram reached Shirdi, he offered the same to Baba. Baba pocketed that rupee and gave another one in return for the sender. Captain Hate's joy knew no bounds when his wish was fulfilled.

There was a 'bhajan' programme at some place. Kamlesh Dhawan was there. She saw someone put a 'rudraksh mala' around the idol of Baba. She yearned for the mala. In no time, the master of the house where the pooja was going on, got up, removed the mala from Baba's neck and offered it to Kamlesh Dhawan.

A nurse wanted to visit Baba's Samadhi Mandir but the head nurse would not sanction her leave. The nurse chanted Baba's name incessantly. The head nurse soon changed her mind and sanctioned the leave.

Sh. C.K. Rajasahib Bahadur was an ardent devotee of Sai Baba. In 1928 he went on a pilgrimage to Dakshineshwar and was keen to see all the places and articles intimately associated with Ram Krishan Paramhans. He especially wanted to see Ram Lalla with whom Ram Krishan Paramhans used to play. The guide showed a huge idol and said that it was Ram Lalla. Sh. Bahadur was not convinced. At this moment, a pujari of the Kali Mandir came out and asked if he was Sh. Bahadur. The pujari said his guru had appeared in his dream and given him Rajasahib's description with the direction to take him around the temple and personally show him everything connected with Ram Krishan Paramhans. See how thoughtful was Baba of his devotees' wishes and desires!

Mrs and Mr V.P. Eyer had six children. While Mrs Eyer stayed at Lucknow to look after the children, the husband, a sugar technologist, worked in different sugar mills. In 1944 he was posted in Kopergaon and there he took every opportunity to be near Sai Baba. In 1945 on 27th May, he was to leave for Lucknow. As two of his sons had come to spend their holidays with their father, he took them to Shirdi on 26th May. The same night he breathed his last! As he always wanted to be near Sai Baba, Sansthan people erected a samadhi for him in the Lendi Bagh.

16

Prayers Answered

*P*rayer is the most potent means of communication between man and God. This means was and is being used all over the world by Sai devotees to solicit divine help.

Mr. Chandorkar, a favourite devotee of Baba, went to a temple in the forest at least ten miles away from the nearest railway station. As the train was late by two hours by the time they (Chandorkar and his party) alighted at the station it was 9p.m. At this time the temple was scheduled to be closed. Chandorkar was tired and hungry. He prayed to Baba that there should a cup of tea at the end of the journey. At 11p.m. when he reached the temple, the pujari was waiting for him with a jug full of tea. The pujari asked him if he was Nana, a name by which Baba used to address him. Chandorkar confirmed his identity and asked the pujari how he knew that he was coming there. The pujari told him that he received an ethereal message from Baba, which said, "My Nana is coming weary, thirsty and hungry. Keep a cup of tea ready for him" The pujari added, "Here is a cup of tea." The prayer was answered with such promptitude!

There was a theft in Rasane's house. His old friend had stolen his wife's jewellery box. He could not report the matter to the police even. So, he wept before Baba's photograph. The next day the man returned the jewellery box and prayed for forgiveness.

Somnath Nimonkar left plague-stricken Pune for his native place Nimon during Christmas of 1917. Gopal, his three year old son, was with him. On the way he halted at Shirdi. When he went to seek permission to proceed, Baba gave him 'udhi' and said, "Go and save the child." Somnath took it as blessings for Gopal. When he reached Nimon his twelve day old nephew was seriously ill. To his dismay he found that he had lost the packet of 'udhi'. So, taking the child in his lap he started praying to Baba very fervently and such is the power of prayer that within fifteen minutes, the child started recovering.

In 1914, Dr. M. R. Tagore was proceeding to the post office to get his War Bonds worth Rs. 2500 encashed. While he was talking with a fellow passenger the bag containing the War Bonds slipped. After some time when the doctor noticed this, he got down from the cart and went back in search of the bag. He walked a mile or so but to no avail. At night, he prayed to Baba for its recovery. Then a voice said to him, "Stop worrying" and peace descended on him and he slept well. In the morning the doctor had to go to a nearby village to attend to a patient. Casually, he talked of the missing bag. There was a girl listening to the doctor. She came with a bag, which she had found on the road. According to her perception there was nothing valuable in the bag. So the bag was intact. The papers had been disturbed, but by God's grace the War Bonds were intact.

Innocent Abdul Kadir of Mumbai was entangled in a criminal case and his wife engaged Raghunath Tendulkar to fight the case. The advocate advised her to appeal to Baba for her innocent husband's acquital. By Baba's grace the man was acquitted in the first hearing.

Once a 'karaka' (penniless) devotee was expected by his 'guru' to bear the expenses of a day's yagna, Rs. 100. So, he went from place to place and performed 'kirtan'. He was promised more than the amount required to be sent to the 'guru'. At the last minute people evaded the payment of the promised sum. He did not know what to do. He sat before Baba's photo and earnestly prayed to Baba for help. For the very next 'kirtan', a devotee gave him Rs. 100 which he could send to the 'guru'. Baba had come to his rescue.

Once Baba gave a four anna coin to Smt. Krishnabai Prabhakar to keep in the pooja room to be worshipped. One day she purchased a coconut for four annas and by mistake gave that coin to the vegetable seller. She repented when she realized the mistake. She prayed to Baba to return the coin to her. In the evening the vegetable seller came and returned the coin.

Abdul was a special 'sevader' of Baba. His son could not be married because he was the son of a faqir. Abdul's mother appealed to Baba for her grandson's marrige as he was being penalized for no fault of his. Baba assured her that He would see to it. In a short time, there came a proposal from a very decent family. They had no objection to Kasim's being a faqir's son as he was an eligible bachelor.

A customs clerk once found certain important documents missing. He was likely to be dismissed if he could not locate them. He prayed to Baba for help. The next day, early in the morning when he reached the office he found the bundle on his table! He was the last to leave and the first to enter the office. He wondered who had come to his help!

Mr. Bhangra, a Parsi, was going by car. On the way the brakes failed. The driver wanted to crash the car against a hillock but he could not do so. As he was a palmist himself, Mr. Bhangra knew for certain that his death was imminent. There were indications of that in his palm. He desperately prayed to Baba to save him for the sake of his family. In no time Baba came to his rescue. One of the tyres of the car burst and the car stopped. The driver changed the tyre and they reached their destination safe and sound.

Mr. B. V. Dev's ten year old son – was down with typhoid. In the course of his illness he cried out one day that gas was rising upward from his belly and pressing hard against his heart. He shouted, "Save me! Save me!". He had become extremely weak from the disease and the father feared even to press his stomach or massage him. He merely cried, "Baba!" in a loud voice. The upward pressure abated at once. That was the shortest prayer ever answered!

In 1928, Mr. Shirian was fined by his superiors on flimsy grounds. At night, he appealed to Baba who assured him that he should not worry. The next day when he went to the office he found that he had been absolved of the charge but an innocent boy had been made the scapegoat. Now Mr. Shirian and the boy prayed to Baba, who told them that the boy's fine would be cancelled on 73rd day. Trusting Baba they did not appeal. Exactly on the 73rd day the boy's fine was cancelled by the same officer who had imposed it.

In 1932 G. B. Dattar misplaced a letter of a travelling client whose presence was urgently required by the court. He tried to find out his whereabouts but in vain. At last, in despair he prayed to Sai Baba. The next day, he chanced to place his hand on the letter. It was on the rack in his office. This helped him to secure the party's presence in time in the court.

Mr. T. R. Eyer's 9 year old daughter was dumb from birth. On 28-3-1942 he went to Shirdi along with his daughter and prayed there. Soon the girl began to cry, "Sai Baba. Sai Baba."

In 1948 Sh. J. M. Munshi, an advocate of Mumbai, was travelling from Banguluru to Mumbai. He was accompanied by his wife. There were six people in the first class compartment, including an old couple and the two youngsters. Four of them started playing cards. The old man was busy praying and his wife was observing them. Some miscreants entered the train. The old man advised them to down the shutters and bolt the doors of their compartment. They did as they were directed to do. For five hours the miscreants went on looting and killing people. But the old man was busy praying fervently. After five hours, they reached a safe station. Theirs was the only compartment, which had been left unscathed. A few days later there was an article in the paper about that incident. The old man had quoted J. M. Munshi's name, so Mr. Munshi's friend came to verify if it was so. The old man had claimed that it was because of his prayer to Shirdi Sai Baba that their compartment had escaped unaffected by the miscreants. Mr. Munshi told his friend that all the facts stated in the article were true. It was also true that theirs was the only compartment which had escaped. It was also true that the old man was praying frantically all the time. He told him that he had never heard of Shirdi Sai Baba before. It was up to him to decide whether the incident was a miracle or a mere coincidence.

Dattatrey Ram Chander, a singer, had a very magical voice, which he lost. In 1951 he went to the Samadhi Mandir at Shirdi and prayed there. To the surprise of all he could sing now!

On 12-5-1973 at midnight a journalist had an attack of paralysis. In the morning he went to the doctor who recommended hospitalization. When he was being taken to the hospital his housekeeper (he was a bachelor.) asked, "When will you be cured?" Though the journalist knew that the disease was incurable and could prove fatal, he said, "In five days' time." In the hospital, he prayed to Baba regularly. On the fifth day he was able to lift his arm and move his fingers. The patient thanked the doctor for restoring his arm but the doctor said that it was not he but Divine Grace, which had done that.

In 1987 Mr. R. P. Kapoor turned 72. Because of an operation he was finding it difficult to walk and even to sit up to pray. On his birthday he prayed to Baba to take him away, as there was no purpose in his life. Two days after the prayer an idea flashed in his mind that he should take 'shilajit'. It had proved ineffective earlier and was lying on the table. He took 'shilajit' and in seven days he was a different man. Was it 'shilajit' that did the wonder? It is for the reader to decide.

In 1933 Dadaji Gopi Nath Joshi with his wife and son was going to Shirdi. At Kopergaon they decided to wade through the Godavari as they thought that the water was very shallow. When they reached the middle of the stream, the force of the current seemed very strong and it seemed that they would be washed away by the current. Gopi Nath felt giddy and closed his eyes and began to pray to Sai Baba for help. Within five minutes Baba Gurav, a servant of Sai Sansthan, came into the middle of the river and helped him through. He helped his wife and son also to cross the river.

Mrs. M. W. Pradhan was in an advanced stage of labour. A midwife and a nurse attended on her. Four days of difficult labour made the nurse despair of her case and she went and told her sister that Mr. Pradhan must send for a doctor at once. But her sister began at once to pray before Baba's portrait with the nurse by her side. As she prayed the child was delivered without any one's help. She and the nurse wondered at how great were Baba's power and mercy.

Mrs Mani Shankar, the famous writer of SAI BABA THE SAINT OF SHIRDI was a fine singer. Once she suffered from a strange congestion in her throat which no medicine could relieve. She could not sing even for a short while. She visited Shirdi and prayed to Baba at the Samadhi Mandir. When she later returned to her room she felt a rustling in her saree. When she took it up she found that it was a packet of Homeopathic tablets. She took it to be as Baba's 'prasad' and soon her throat was cleared of the congestion.

Though Mr. Virandra Pandya had no faith in Baba, he visited Shirdi with his brothers. Once when his family had to face many difficulties he took out the picture of Baba which was lying in his trunk, kept it in the shrine and prayed fervently that he should find a solution to his problem by that evening. Soon an idea came to him and after that peace descended on him. Strangely, he learnt from a letter that the same solution had occurred to his mother too, precisely at the same hour. He now decided to dedicate all his life to Baba, giving up all worldly activities. But his mother insisted that he should marry. Again he prayed for a written solution to his problem. The next day his eyes fell on a book entitled SRI SAI BABA UPASANA. He opened it at random and the chapter BHAVSUDHA came up. The message contained was that a householder's life is preferable. Yet he doubted whether it was a mere coincidence.

At that time he was residing in a forest area infested by robbers masquerading as sadhus. So, he had instructed his watchman not to permit even sadhus to enter his gate. With these facts in mind, one day he prayed, "Baba, tomorrow is Thursday, a day sacred to you. Let a sadhu come at lunch time and bless me by keeping his right hand on my head. He should pass his hand over my whole body. If this is granted, my faith in You will be strengthened and I vow I will visit Shirdi."

The next day at lunch time no sadhu turned up. Just as Pandya was about to partake of the first morsel, a sadhu called for food. When Pandya offered him food the former received the same and put his right hand on Pandya's head by way of blessing and left. Pandya recognized that only a part of his wish was fulfilled and that he had not received the sadhu in a proper manner. While he was thinking this, the sadhu returned. Pandya offered Him Rs. 2 as 'dakshina'. The Faqir passed his hand all over Pandya's body, smiled sportingly and went away. The next Thursday Pandya fulfilled his vow.

Udhi and Prayer to Cure

Arthur Osborne says that it was in the healing of the sick that Sai Baba's powers were most lavishly displayed. If 'udhi' by itself was not enough, the power of prayer was added to it and the two together worked wonders.

To record all Sai Baba's miraculous cures would be an impossible task but still an attempt is being made to record some of them.

Allergy
Mrs Vimal Kesar who lived in Germany, had an eight-year-old daughter, whose skin was allergic to pollen and animals. Her sister from Mumbai sent her 'udhi' to be applied on the affected parts and it improved her condition but did not cure her fully. The family visited Shirdi and placed a letter of prayer written by the girl at Sai Baba's feet. She took 'udhi' orally and applied it on the body. Within two months the girl was fully cured of her allergy.

Illness
In 1985 J.P. Sawant's fifteen-year-old son was to appear in an examination. Just a day before that he fell ill. His mother prayed to Baba for help and gave 'udhi' to the son. The next day he was able to appear in the examination and ultimately got through.

Lump in the breast
In 1986 a Sai sevika developed a big lump in her right breast. The doctors advised removal of the breast by surgery but the lady

could not reconcile to the idea of surgery. She went to the nearby Sai temple and told the pujari about her problem. The pujari recommended applying 'udhi' paste five times a day after reading *Sai Mahima*. He also suggested sesame oil massage on Mondays, Tuesdays and Thursdays after chanting Om Sai 108 times. The lady carried out the instructions and visited the Samadhi Mandir. On her return from Shirdi she noticed that the lump had started reducing. On 12 October1986 she was completely cured of the lump.

Delivery

Rajballi Mohd. Khoja's buffalo had great trouble in calving. He sent for the veterinary surgeon who tried his best especially as Khoja was the chairman of the Sanitary Committee of the Municipality. But he was of not much help. Khoja thought of 'udhi' and applied it on the buffalo's forehead and prayed to Baba for help. Within ten minutes she safely calved. There was no more trouble.

18

Udhi, Prayer and Dream to Cure

*B*aba was a very unique doctor. If 'udhi' and prayer could not cure any patient he appeared in the dream of the patient and cured him/her.

Stones in the Gall Bladder

Shyamla of Chennai developed severe pain in the abdomen. The X-ray showed stones in the gall bladder. Hence surgery was recommended. There was a Sai devotee in her neighbourhood. She sought his guidance. The neighbour had a vision of Baba who told him that surgery was not required and that she should drink more milk and eat less solid food. She followed Baba's instructions, conveyed through her neighbour and in addition she took a pinch of 'udhi'. A month of this medicine completely cured her of gall bladder stones.

Eczema

In 1929, one Appaji Sutar of Shirdi was suffering from eczema. He went to the Kopergaon hospital and then to the Nasik hospital for treatment but it had no effect. He spent a lot of money on his treatment. It was his eighth day in the hospital when Baba appeared in his dream and instructed him to go back to Shirdi, read the *Vishnu Puran* and apply 'udhi'. He hesitated as he was still under treatment. Baba repeated his instructions and he had to obey. In a week's time he was fully cured! There was no trace of the disease on the skin.

Measles, Pneumonia and Abscess

In 1934, Sh. Deshmukh's son had measles, pneumonia and an abscess on the chest. The doctor was afraid to operate upon the child as he was very weak. So Sh. Deshmukh depended on his doctor, Sai Baba and His sanjivani. He applied 'udhi' on the abscess and prayed to Baba. A friend who was watching him asked him whether 'udhi' could cure him.

'Yes,' replied Sh. Deshmukh.

'In how much time?' asked his friend in jest.

'Twenty-four hours,' said Deshmukh.

That night Baba appeared in his dream and chided him, "Why did you say twenty-four hours? You should have said, 'Immediately.'" By the next morning the child was healed.

Fits

Sh. V.N. Murthy Rao of Bangalore started having fits at the age of nineteen and this went on for seventeen years. In 1943, a friend of his gave him 'udhi' and asked him to pray to Baba. He did as he was directed and the fits became fewer and milder. His mother was anxious that he should get cured quickly. So she approached a 'tantrik'. Baba appeared in her dream and promised to cure him within three – four months. The man was cured during that period.

Throat Cancer

Mrs Sneh Kiran's maternal uncle went to Chandigarh for the treatment of throat cancer. There he was introduced to Baba through his niece. He was so enamoured of Baba that he started taking and applying 'udhi' on the affected part. He started chanting Baba's name. By the time he went to the hospital for treatment he had been cured of his fatal disease. During this period he had two dreams. In one of the dreams he felt that he had been bound and felt suffocated. He thought that his end was near, so he started chanting Baba's name. In the second dream Baba appeared before him and placed His loving hand on his head. His cancer was cured.

Udhi as Annapurna

Udhi has been frequently used for medical purposes. But Sh. Brahmdev Upadhyay of Kolkata used it for a different purpose. There was a 'greh pravesh' function at his house. Seventy to eighty guests were expected. Arrangement was made for ninety to hundred people. But the number of guests went up to 150. What was to be done? Mrs Upadhyaya put some 'udhi' into the dishes, covered them and prayed to Baba for help. Such was Baba's grace that there was still food in the dishes when the guests had eaten .

There was a funeral feast at Mrs Nawaskar's house. The guests who turned up were more than expected. The lady of the house was worried. Her mother-in-law suggested to her to put 'udhi' in the food and keep the vessels covered when serving. She did as she was advised and she found to her surprise and joy that not only was the food sufficient to feed all the guests but plenty of it remained after all the guests had eaten.

20

Baba's Appearance

Baba appeared before people in different forms, sometimes as a leper, at times as a faqir or even as a Bhil. At times He even appeared as Baba Himself. Arthur Osborne says that to people who had seen Him He usually appeared in a strange form whereas to those who had not, He more often appeared in His own form as though considering the additional work of disguise unnecessary.

Baba as leper

On a certain Thursday, Baba appeared to a devotee in the form of a leper with a begging bowl. The moment the devotee put his hand into his pocket Baba disappeared. Efforts to trace him proved futile.

In 1936, Narsimha Swami went to Sakori to pay his respects to Upasani Baba. Ram Babu was also there. Upasani Baba had arranged for an open feast. At the end of the feast there came a leper who had a frightful appearance. He had one eye. Pus and blood were oozing out of his disfigured lips, nose and eyes. A foul smell was emanating from his body. As he could not feed himself, Upasani Baba asked Ram Babu to feed the leper with his own hands. He obeyed Upasani Baba but took care to see that his hands did not touch the leper. The result was some of the food kept spilling. When after eating the leper had gone, Upasani Baba asked Narsimha Swami to eat the remnants of the contaminated food. He ate it up without any hesitation. Everyone present there was amazed. Then Upasani Baba said, "Did you see how quickly the old man walked away? Do you know who came in the garb of a repulsive leper? It was none other than Baba Himself.'

Baba as a faqir

In 1917, Anna Sahib Kulkarani was away when a faqir visited his house and gave 'udhi' to his wife. When asked if he was Sai Baba the faqir replied that he was an obedient servant of Sai Baba. Mrs Kulkarani gave the faqir one rupee as dakshina. When Mr Kulkarani returned and came to know about it he said that he would have given ten rupees and not one to that faqir resembling Sai Baba. He searched for him and found him. He gave him one rupee but the faqir wanted more. He gave two rupees more but the faqir still wanted more. Again he gave him three rupees but he was not satisfied. Then he took out a ten-rupee note and gave it to him. The faqir accepted the tenner and returned all the coins he had received from him. This was precisely the amount that Mr Kulkarani had said he would have given were he present when the faqir visited their house. Still greater surprise was in store for the Kulkarani family. When they opened the packet of 'udhi', miraculously it had turned into akshat.

In 1955, at lunch time a faqir came to the house of Jai Ram Raje. He was dressed like a Muslim. Raje, being an orthodox Brahmin, offered him food on a leaf and asked him to eat it elsewhere. But the faqir insisted on sitting there. After lunch, the faqir demanded dakshina. Raje said that if a client paid him fifty rupees he would give him his due. The faqir said that the client would pay him at 3.15 p.m. and that he himself would return at 5 p.m. to receive the dakshina. To Mr Raje's surprise the client turned up at 3.15 p.m. sharp! The faqir, too, came at 5 p.m. to collect his due and received ten rupees. In return the latter gave him 'udhi'. By the time it fell into his hand, it got mysteriously transformed into a rose! Raje looked up in surprise but the faqir was not to be seen anywhere.

In 1966, Mr Chitnis was to go to Agra by car. He prayed to Baba for his darshan. On the way the car stopped at a place for no apparent reason. A faqir who resembled Sai Baba was found standing nearby. The faqir blessed them and received 'dakshina.' Mr Chitnis was surprised to know later that only his youngest son, he and the driver saw the faqir and others did not see him.

Baba as pilgrims

Upasani Baba was forbidden to leave Shirdi, but he was adamant about returning home. Sai Baba challenged that he could not go. On the way at Kopergaon temple, the pujari advised him to go back to Shirdi but he would not listen to him. At that time there came some pilgrims who wanted a guide for Shirdi. The pujari recommended Upasani Baba for that. Upasani Baba had to accompany the pilgrims. However when he reached Shirdi the pilgrims disappeared. Upasani was back in Shirdi.

Baba as Baba

Mhalsapathy went on a pilgrimage to Jajori in a palanquin and a few companions. There, they came to know that there was an outbreak of plague. So they were sad and dejected. Mhalsapathy stood there dumb and sad leaning against the palanquin. Suddenly he felt someone was standing behind him. When he turned he found Baba who, at once, disappeared. Now, Mhalsapathy was emboldened because Sai Baba was with him and so they stayed there for four days and returned to Shirdi safe and sound. When Mhalsapathy went to the Dwarkamai Sai Baba smiled and said, "Bhakt, you had a fine journey? When you stood leaning against the palanquin I came there."

One morning, Megha worshipped Baba as usual and was lying awake with his eyes shut. Baba entered his room, sprinkled akshat at him and asked him to draw a trident. When Megha opened his eyes he found akshat, no doubt, but Baba had come and gone through the closed door.

Mr U. Shirinasmurthy as a boy had accompanied his friend to a neighbouring village. On the way in a bush, he found a small stone idol. Curiously, they looked at it closely. It was the figure of a man and he had a headdress and a beard. One of his legs was resting across the other. He went and picked it up and then he forgot all about this incident. During his college days when he first saw the picture of Sai Baba, he, at once, remembered the stone idol he had picked up in his boyhood. It was 9 p.m. when he returned to his room. He opened the door and was terrified at what he saw. His heart missed a beat and his legs shivered. It was as if he were rooted to the ground. There before his very eyes was Sai Baba, resting on the mat with his head on his forearm. In the midst of the fright a doubt arose in his mind whether that was a mere illusion. He, at once, closed his eyes and opened them again. It was not an illusion. Sai Baba Himself was there.

21

Baba as a Unique Doctor

We know that whether it was during His life time or after his 'mahasmadhi' Baba took different forms to alleviate the sufferings of the ailing humanity.

DELIVERY

Mr. Chandorkar's pregnant daughter was having a difficult delivery. Baba knew that Chandorkar needed help. He sent a messenger with 'udhi'. The messenger was reluctant as he did not have enough money to cover the rail and road journey. Baba coaxed him to go promising that everything would be taken care of. When the messenger alighted at the station it was night time and he didn't have money to engage a conveyance. Suddenly there appeared a liveried peon shouting his name. He had brought a 'tonga' for him. So, without any hassle he reached Mr. Chandorkar's house and delivered the 'udhi'. The 'udhi' showed its miracle when it was applied on the forehead of the patient. After the delivery when the situation became calm, the messenger came out to thank the 'tongawala', but the 'tonga' and the 'tongawala' had disappeared. Then, he went to Mr. Chandorkar to thank him for sending the 'tonga' which had brought him to his residence. He was surprised to know that Mr. Chandorkar had not sent any 'tonga' as he did not know that a messenger was coming to his house. Both of them realized that it was Baba who had provided the 'tonga' and the 'tongawala'.

Gopichand, a famous writer, was an atheist. Once his wife was in hospital and had been suffering from labour pains for three days and her condition was critical. On the third day as he passed by the Sai Mandir, on the way to the hospital, he thought, " Baba, if You could bless my wife with a safe delivery I shall believe that Your power is divine." At the hospital at that time his wife delivered a male child. She told him that an old man sat on her bed and said, " Don't be afraid. I shall save you." In a vision, He then smeared a little 'udhi' on her forehead, put a little of it in water and gave it to her to drink. She delivered at once. The time of this vision coincided precisely with the time of his silent prayer to Baba. Gopichand named his son Sai Baba causing quite a stir among his atheist friends.

OPERATION

In 1909 Balwant Nachane's elder brother was undergoing a throat operation in a hospital at Mumbai. Naturally, the whole family at Dahanu was anxious about him. At noon a 'sadhu' appeared in front of their house and asked for food. They received him with due respect and fed him well but did not serve him 'bhindi bhaji' as they thought it was too poor a dish for such a revered guest. But he especially asked for it and was served. Then, he said that the operation at the hospital had been completed quite satisfactorily and went away. Hari Bhau, a friend of Nachane expressed the hope that by Sai Baba's grace it might be so. That was the first time that Nachane ever heard the name of Sai Baba.

In the evening Nachane's father returned from the hospital and told the people at home that the operation was successful and that soon after the operationa, a 'sadhu' had approached the patient and passing his hands over the operated portion had said that all would be well and had gone away.

In 1912, Nachane visited Shirdi. One day pointing to him, Baba said, "I have been to this man's house for a meal and he did not give Me 'bhindi bhaji'. Nachane's mind went back to the incident of 1909 and he realized that Sai Baba had graced his house in the form of a 'sadhu' even before the family ever heard of Him. What surprised Nachane was that Sai Baba did not at all resemble the 'sadhu' whom he had observed quite closely.

In 1912, Rao Bahadur S. B. Dhumal underwent an operation. But he saw Baba seated on a chair close to the operation table before the chloroform began to take effect. As Baba was there to look after him, he felt reassured. The operation was a success.

Dr. Iqbal Singh Sahni went to London for his treatment. His operation was successful but there were post operational problems. One night, Mrs. Sahni prayed to Sai Baba for help. That night Baba appeared in London and talked to the nurse on night duty and gave certain instructions to her in English. The next day, the nurse pointing to the photo which the Sahnis had placed in the room told Mrs. Sahni, "This gentleman, a relative of yours, had come to see Mr. Iqbal Singh Sahni and enquired about his health." Tears trickled from Mrs. Sahni's eyes. From then onwards Mr. Iqbal Singh started recovering.

BREATHING TROUBLE

Kashinath (Upasani Baba) had breathing trouble. The visible effect of this was that his belly had grown big. An old man met him and told him, "Drink water as hot as your tongue can tolerate. Avoid cold water and you will recover." Kashinath brushed aside this advice. When he was going to the river to drink water, the old man suddenly appeared before him and admonished him for ignoring his advice. He commanded him to take hot water and vanished as mysteriously as he had appeared. Amazed at the incident Kashinath heeded the warning and within three weeks his condition improved a lot. But he wanted to be fully cured. Again on the advice of Yogi Kulkarani visited Shirdi on 27-6-1911 and in a trice his complaint disappeared. Sitting in the Dwarkamai, looking at Kashinath, Baba said to the gathering that once He saw a pregnant woman who did not deliver the child even after years of pregnancy. Later, He advised her to drink only hot water, which would help her in an easy delivery. The lady ignored the advice and approached a stream to drink water. Baba fearing that she would unnecessarily die along with all the infants in her belly, again approached her and admonished her to take hot water. So she did and got relief immediately. Kashinath knew for certain that Baba was referring to him.

Four and a half year old Suhas had breathing trouble, which would get aggravated at night. When physicians failed to cure him, he was hospitalized. One night the child had a vision. He saw Sai Baba. He asked the doctor to vacate the seat for Baba. The doctor could not believe it. He thought the child was delirious. But the child insisted that Baba was standing near the doctor. During the last three weeks the doctors had not been able to diagnose the disease but that day they could diagnose a minor problem, which they were able to cure.

TUBERCULOSIS

In 1948, Sh. Kasavaya Vaidya was diagnosed as having tuberculosis. On 10th June he went to Chennai for treatment. The doctors there found his case hopeless. He knew for certain that he was not going to live. On 24-4-49 at about 11:30 a.m. Kasavaya clearly saw "Yamdooth" entering his room. Unperturbed, he said to them mentally, "You can take me away after securing the permission of Sai Baba." At once Baba appeared on the scene and drove them out. The very next moment loud wailing was heard from the neighbouring house. An ailing person in that house had passed away. But Mr. Kasavaya's condition improved rapidly from then onward.

ILL HEALTH

Miss Dutton, a Christian, was leaving the convent for Calcutta due to ill health. In her closed house appeared a Faqir who demanded money. Miss Duttaon said that she had no money. But the Faqir pointed to the thirty rupees she had kept in the cupboard and had forgotten. When she turned to give the money the Faqir had disappeared. But after that she felt at peace. In Calcutta, she told her neighbour about her experience. The neighbour showed her a photo of Baba. She instantly recognized Him to be the same Faqir whom she had seen in the convent.

PARALYSIS / POLIO

A hotel owner of Shirdi had a paralytic daughter who was taken to the Samadhi Mandir and laid there. Within a few minutes she was seen getting up and going around the 'Samadhi.' Later she told her astonished parents that she saw Baba telling her to get up and walk and she found that she could get up and walk.

In 1933-34 Ramchander Vasudeva Chaisa's wife had a serious attack of paralysis. Her life appeared to be in danger. But she was a staunch believer of Sai Baba. She had a vision and in it she saw Baba sitting at the doorway of the room and telling her, "I am here to guard you. I will not allow even the 'yamdooths' to enter." She also saw some men bringing bamboos, an earthern pot, etc and preparing a bier to carry her corpse. But Baba asked them to clear off and when they did not listen to Him, He kicked them away and broke their bamboos and the earthern pot. The same night a person in the opposite house died. But his wife's life was saved and she recovered soon.

In 1956, a widowed school teacher's sixteen year old son appeared for SSC examination but when he returned from the examination hall, he had a very serious attack of fever. Medicines could cure his fever but not the lameness, which the fever brought with it. In fact, he was afflicted with polio. His mother took him to Shirdi but she had to go to the Samadhi Mandir alone to pray as the boy had to be carried around by a hired person and he felt too shy to go there. He found it very embarrassing and stayed back in their room and asked his mother to carry on with her devotion. One day, Baba appeared before the boy physically, lifted him by the hand and led him to the Samadhi Mandir. Then, Baba told him to stand leaning against a pillar. When the lady went back to the Wada, the boy was not there. She came back to the Samadhi Mandir in a panic. To her pleasant surprise the boy was standing leaning against a pillar. She could not believe it when the boy narrated the incident. But it was a fact that he was able to walk and in a month's time he was fully cured.

DIARRHOEA

In 1955 Mrs. Sushilamma suffered from diarrhoea. All medical aid proved futile. She was too weak even to go out of the room to answer the call of nature. One day, when she got up for that purpose she prayed to Baba for help. Baba, at once, entered the room and asked her to wear a talisman, which He had kept on the shelf. The people in her house did not believe this but when they searched on the shelf, there was a talisman. She put it around her neck. At once, her diarrhea subsided.

STOMACHACHE

It was a Tuesday of June 1960. Mr. Nemichand Jain was sitting in his shop. A tall well-built Faqir stood in front of his shop asking for five annas. Mr. Jain could find only four annas and the Faqir would not accept a penny less. When Mr. Jain was searching for the fifth anna, the Faqir said, "Aren't you suffering from severe stomachache?" Mr. Jain was surprised as it was a fact. The Faqir gave Mr. Jain 'udhi' to eat and apply on the forehead and this was to cure him of his pain in two days time. Now, the Faqir enhanced His fee by Re 1 and four annas. While Mr. Jain was searching for the exact amount, the Faqir disappeared. As predicted by the Faqir, by Thursday Mr. Jain was cured of his disease. In August 1960 Mr. Jain visited Shirdi. He found the same Faqir sitting on the throne of the Samadhi Mandir. As soon as one rupee and four annas were offered to Him, He changed into a beautiful marble statue of Baba.

UTERINE TUMOUR

Mrs. Mehboob was suffering from uterine tumour. In September 1982, she was admitted into a hospital for an operation. Mr. Mehboob thought of invoking divine help as a last resort. He prayed to Baba, "Am I to be a widower at this stage and the children to be motherless? Lord save me from this." The next moment some one patted him from behind. When he turned back, he saw a tall old man in a clean white dress and He assured him with these words. "Nothing amiss will happen to your wife. Don't worry." As he stepped into the hospital room, to his amazement the hospital staff told him that the crisis had passed and his wife was out of danger. Shortly after that the young wife started regaining her health. Mr. Mehboob realized that Baba had come to his rescue to save his wife.

PNEUMONIA

Dattatrey Vithal Vaidya says that once his father had a very severe attack of pneumonia. It was 21st day of fever. At 9 p.m his father cried that Baba had come. He wanted them to bring bread and onion for Him. But everyone including the doctors thought that he was delirious and did not do what he asked of them. His father got angry and asked them to quit the room. They had to obey him but they could know what went on inside the hospital room. They could overhear the conversation going on between Baba and his father. They could hear Baba asking two persons to leave and they were not willing to leave without his father. Then Baba struck His 'sataka' (rod) on the floor and they left. Baba asked his father to drink plenty of cold water!. His father wanted cold water but they could not give cold water to a pneumonia patient. After much persuasion, his mother gave his father as much cold water as he wanted. The temperature came down. By the next day, the patient was declared to be out of danger.

In 1930, Dr. Rustamji was laid up with pneumonia and was admitted in a hospital in Mumbai. The doctors gave up hope as he was in coma. A Faqir appeared to him in a vision and said, "Let your health recover first. Later you will come to know Me." He went round Rustamji's cot and then disappeared. Soon after that the doctors were surprised to find that his condition was quite normal. Ever since then Rustamji yearned to meet the Faqir. Six months had passed, a passenger who sat next to him in the bus was reading a book on Sai Baba. Rustamji saw Baba's picture in it and realized that He was the Faqir who had saved him and started reading about Sai Baba. Soon after that he was appointed as a doctor in the Sai Baba Sansthan Dispensary at Shirdi.

SCIATICA

In 1912, Mr. G. K. Rege was down with sciatica. In that condition he went to his father-in-law's house. His father-in law, a Sai devotee, applied 'udhi' on his forehead. On that very afternoon, when he was relaxing on a cot he saw a 'sanyasi' telling him that he would be all right in three days. He shouted to his father-in-law and told him whom he had seen and what He was telling him. The moment his father-in-law came the 'sanyasi' disappeared. But exactly on the third day his pain left him and within a week he was all right.

CHOLERA

Raghubir Purandhar of Bandra, Mumbai, records his experience of Baba's appearance before him away from Shirdi. He says, "My wife had an attack of cholera and the doctors had given her up as a gone case. Then I saw Baba standing by the side of Dattatrey Mandir in front of my house and He ordered me to give her 'udhi' and 'tirath' so I gave her the same. Half an hour later she recovered sufficient warmth of body and the doctors felt hopeful of her recovery and she recovered soon.

FEVER

Raoji Balkrishan Upasani's 5 – 6 year old son was down with high fever. Several medicines were tried but they failed to bring the temperature down. Even the doctors felt it was a hopeless case. Each day Raoji used to keep awake, sitting near the boy's bed. Then, one day in the early hours of the morning, while Raoji was feeling a bit drowsy Baba came near the boy and applied 'udhi' on his forehead and said, "Don't worry now. He will be all right within two hours. He will perspire but wipe it away." Hearing these words he suddenly came to himself and looked for Baba in the room but found no trace of Him around. No doubt 'udhi' had been applied on the patient's forehead. Within a short time, the sick boy began to perspire. And as he perspired more and more, his fever came down. Four days later Raoji left for Shirdi with his son. The 'tongawala' did not turn up at the appointed time so he was late in reaching Shirdi. As a rule, he should have missed the 'arati' but 'the arati'

Baba as a Unique Doctor

was yet to start. Baba had said, "Wait for some time. Your Dhulia friend will be coming here soon. (Raoji belonged to Dhulia) So the 'arati' started when Raoji reached the Mosque. Baba took Raoji's son by his side and asked the boy, "You remember I had come to your house when you were sick?"

CONVULSIONS

One night four hours after sunset Chhotubai Pradhan was about to fall asleep. Baba appeared before her and said, "Why are you sleeping? Get up. Your boy will have convulsions." Then she got up and looked at the boy who was sleeping by her side without any fever or trouble. But since she had clearly heard the words from Baba and she thought to be forewarned is to be forearmed. She got up and lighted a fire, heated water and kept eu de cologne and other domestic medicines ready by the bed. Then at two in the morning her son woke up and started convulsing. But since she had kept all the medicines ready at hand, and he was given the necessary treatment and his fits soon disappeared.

SERIOUS ILLNESS

R. K. Dube who had vowed to go to Shirdi broke his promise and went somewhere else instead. On that trip he lost his child and his wife became seriously ill again. He prayed to Baba for her recovery. Baba appeared in a vision to him and said, "One must fulfil one's vow otherwise one has to pay the penalty." Then after applying 'udhi' on Mrs. Dube's face and forehead Baba disappeared. Dube saw the 'udhi' on his wife's face and forehead. After some days when Mrs. Dube was able to travel, they went to Shirdi to thank Baba for her recovery. There Baba remarked that He had gone and applied 'udhi' on his wife's face and forehead.

Kaka Dixit once received a letter from Nagpur which informed him that his brother who had been sick, was seriously ill now. It further requested him to come to Nagpur to look after his ailing brother. With that letter in hand Kaka Dixit went to the Mosque and said, " Baba, I am sorry. I am of no service to him." At this

Baba remarked, "But I am of service." Kaka Dixit wasn't given leave to go to Nagpur nor could Kaka understand what Baba meant by "I am of service." After a couple of days, Kaka received another letter from Nagpur, which intimated him that on that very day and about the same time when in the Mosque at Shirdi, Baba had said those cryptic words, an unknown sadhu had come to his brother's house and cured his brother's illness, uttering the same words which Baba had said to Kaka when he had requested leave to go Nagpur.

Wonderful were the life and ways of Sai Baba and more wonderful the way in which He cured His men. He transferred the devotees' ailments onto Himself and some times He prescribed some extraordinary recipe and at times He cured them with His kind blessings or by His mere glance. The remedies He resorted to ward off killer epidemics like plague which ravaged the country, in His time, were simple, uncommon, extraordinary and extremely bizarre.

Baba was in fact, a unique doctor. It is said Baba used to take the juice of any leaf He found nearby and give it as medicine. Whatever seed He found, He used to ask the patient to make a paste of it and use it as medicine. If He touched the ailing limb of a patient, the ailment would disappear. Slowly, people recognized Him as a great physician. So many and so varied were the cures experienced by His devotees that it is impossible to catalogue them all. Sometimes He appeared in person to cure His devotees and sometimes the application of 'udhi' was enough. Some devotees were cured of their ailments by merely keeping His picture.

LAMENESS

When Baba went to Dhoopkhera with Chand Patil, He threw stones at the advancing crowd, which would not allow them to proceed further. He threw stones all round. A stone hit a lame boy. The agonized mother ran to his rescue but when she picked up the boy, there were no marks of injury or bleeding. He stood erect! His lameness was gone.

Baba as a Unique Doctor

Shankar Keshav Bhatt, a shopkeeper of Mumbai tried several medicines and several doctors, big and small, to find a cure for the pain in his leg but was unable to find any relief. His leg gave him unbearable pain for many years. He could walk only a couple of steps that too with extreme difficulty. Then he heard of Baba and went to Shirdi to have His 'darshan' and to get a cure. For two days he stayed in Shirdi and on the third day he left Shirdi with Baba's blessings and 'udhi'. But he was still limping. Since it was the rainy season and the Godawari deep, one had to catch a ferry and then cross over to Kopergaon side. Before boarding the ferry one had to walk some distance from the place where the tonga stopped up to the water flow. At Shirdi, when S. K. Bhatt, had got into the tonga to go home there was intense pain in his leg and he could hardly walk and on the Godawari bank while getting down, he slipped. He fell down and cried in pain and the men who had come with him in the tonga rushed to him and helped him get up and stand and then there was Baba's wonder cure! The moment he fell the sprain and the pain left him. Bhatt himself walked without limping and jumped into the ferry.

Dixit Kaka was at Shirdi. He was suffering from pain in the leg. He found it hard to walk even a furlong. One evening, Baba started for Neemgaon. Dixit accompanied Him. Though they walked together for three miles, Dixit suffered no pain.

Dr. Chimdamber Pillay suffered much from pain caused by guinea worms in his leg. The pain was so unbearable that the doctor preferred death to sufferings. He knew his sufferings were due to his actions in the past but requested Baba through Kaka Dixit to end his pain and transfer the fruits of his 'karma' to ten of his future lives. When Kaka Dixit told Baba the doctor's wish Baba said to him, "Let him cast away his fear. Why should he suffer for ten more births when he could live out the fruits of his 'karma' within ten days. When I am here he need not pray to die. Bring him here and I will finish his sufferings here and now." Then the doctor was lifted from his lodgings, taken to the Mosque and placed by Baba's side. Baba gave him a bolster to lean on and relax and said to the doctor, "Take rest and don't worry. One has to suffer for one's 'karma'. Remember God will take care of you. Surrender yourself at His feet and see how He will immediately come to your help. A crow will come and peck at your leg and then after that you will recover and your sufferings will come to an end." When Baba and Dr, Pillay were talking Abdul who cleaned the Mosque and trimmed the lamps came and started trimming the lamps. Accidentally he set his foot on the doctor's outstretched leg that was all swollen. All the seven guinea worms which were eating the doctor's flesh and drinking his blood, were squeezed out in that instant. Unable to bear the sudden pain Dr. Pillay shrieked in extreme anguish and began weeping. After some time the doctor calmed down and started singing in joy. Then Baba exclaimed, "Look, Bhau is all right now. So he is singing in utter joy." When the doctor asked Baba when the crow would come Baba told him, "Didn't you see the crow, dear doctor? Abdul was the crow and he will not come to you again. Go and rest in the Wada and you will soon be all right."

MADNESS OR MENTAL ILLNESS

At Dhoopkhera Baba was throwing stones at the crowd. A stone hit a young girl who moved about naked, being of unsound mind. One of the stones hit her on the forehead. Her mother ran to her rescue but the girl disappeared into her house and hurriedly put on her clothes to cover her naked body. Gone was her madness. She became normal.

Rambaji, a devotee from Nasik, was mentally ill when he came to Shirdi. He used to drink 'tirath', (water in which Baba had taken a bath) and this cured his illness.

In 1913 after the doctors' medicines and treatment had proved in vain, a Parsi gentleman took his lunatic brother to Shirdi. As the patient showed improvement within a day or two they returned to Bombay. But after their return the malady struck the man again and he started to behave abnormally and trouble his people. So the younger brother took him to Shirdi and left him there on Baba's advice. After some months' stay, merely by attending Baba's 'aratis' and taking His 'udhi' and 'tirath' and by His looks of grace, that man soon regained his reasoning power and his lunacy was gone.

PLAGUE

In 1911, Waman Rao Patel (Swami Sharan Anand) of Mumbai came on his first visit to Baba. Plague was preying on Shirdi and seven buboes of the epidemic had appeared on Baba's body. When the devotees asked Him what medicines they should give Him to relieve Him of the bubonic pains, Baba told them, "Don't worry. These buboes on My body simply signify the death of seven persons here. Then they will go." As the devotees pressed Him to have the buboes treated He asked them to apply burnt cotton soaked in oil on them. This was done. As soon as seven persons died of plague, buboes from Baba's body disappeared.

Mrs. Kharparde's son was stricken with plague. She went to Sai Baba to seek His permission to leave Shirdi so that her son could get medical aid at their home-town. Baba lifted His robe and there were egg-sized bumps on His body. Baba told her that He had taken the killer disease on Himself. No other traditional medical treatment was given to Kharparde's son. He got well automatically.

EYE-TROUBLE

Baba's cures for ailments of the sick were miraculous, no doubt, but His methods were different and unconventional. He cured the inflammation of Shyama's eyes by applying pepper!. Ramgir Bua says that when Baba Himself got inflammation of the eyes and they were looking red, He pounded pepper into paste and applied that pepper-paste on His eye-lids and He was cured.

Sometimes Baba used extremely unconventional methods to cure a patient. It is said that in one case when a patient came to Him with a diseased eye, He pulled out the eye ball, cleaned, and reinserted it! Truly, a surgical feat unheard of any where in the world.

Mrs. Manager had eye trouble. Her eyes were paining constantly. Once when she was sitting in the Dwarkamai Baba cast a glance on her. Instantly her eyes stopped paining and watering. But Baba's eyes had taken on the trouble from her. It was a wonderful way of treating a patient, without any medicine.

Mr. Kalekar's grand daughter was crying on account of severe pain in the eyes. Baba asked him to foment her eyes with an onion. Baba's treatment never failed!

Once, a lady devotee of Baba suffered from severe pain in her eyes. Doctors examined her and declared that even doctors abroad would not be able to help her. The husband brought her to Shirdi and every day he used to take her around Baba's Samadhi. She promised to offer an embroidered shawl to Baba's palaquin if she was cured. In the course of a year she was all right and she fulfilled her vow.

BLINDNESS

Yashwant Deashpande, Vithal Deshpande's father, had lost his sight due to old age but he had a strong desire to go to Shirdi and bow to Baba. As his son was busy, he asked his grandson to accompany him to Shirdi and thus at last he came to Shirdi. While prostrating the old man said to Baba, "Baba, I am sorry. I can't see You, " to which Baba said, "Of course, you will be able to see." Meanwhile the boy had gone to the lodging to bring the purse which he had forgotten there. Baba passed His hand over the old man's eyes and at once his blindness was gone and his sight restored. Then Yashwant left the Mosque with Baba's permission and 'udhi' while his grandson returned to the Mosque and not finding his grandfather there, he ran about in the village searching for him. He found him at last in their lodging quite safe, having walked all the distance from the Mosque all alone.

One day, a blind man came and sat in the shade of the tree where Baba was meditating. A few rowdies came and manhandled the blind man. This disturbed Baba's meditation. He came to know the reason of the commotion. Feeling pity for the blind man Baba with His divine hands cleaned both his eyes and holding the eyelids firmly with His hands, He passed divine rays from His eyes into those of the blind man. Unable to bear the agony of the burning eyes the blind man cried aloud and fainted. The rowedies who had ill-treated the blind man, earlier assembled there with some others. After a short time the blind man regained his consciousness and found that he was no longer blind!

Shyama's uncle had a blind grandfather. Shyama led him to Baba . Baba simply laid His hand on the old man's head and his eyesight was restored.

HEADACHE

Once a lady from Bandra, Mumbai, who had been suffering from severe headache for the last seven years, came to Shirdi for the first time. Baba touched and pressed her head very gently and asked her if she had a headache. She replied that she had it when she came but it had vanished since Baba patted her head.

Purandhar was suffering from an unbearable headache for a long time. He sent word to Baba through Dr. Pillay that it would be better for him to end his life rather than be subjected to such pain. Baba sent him a snuff-like substance, which immediately cured his headache.

For nearly a month, Tarabai Tarkhand (popularly known as Mrs. Manager) suffered from a severe headache. She tried many medicines but none could give her any relief and she felt that she might die. With that feeling she left for Shirdi so that she might have the special benefit of dying at Baba's feet. In spite of objections by her husband and others, they got down at Kopergaon, and came to the Godawari which they had to cross. There it suddenly struck that lady that she should have a dip in the holy river. She thought she was going to die very soon and the cold bath might increase the pain and accelerate her death. She didn't fear death. Knowing she would die, she took her bath and to their wonder when she came out of the cold water of the Godawari, her headache was gone and she was reborn!

BODYACHE

When Mrs. Septnaker bowed to Baba, He said, "My arms, My abdomen and My waist had been paining for a long time. I have tried many medicines in vain. But to My utter surprise all the pains have gone just now." It indeed was Mrs. Septnaker's story. She was cured of all the pains from which she had been suffering for a long time. She was amazed at Baba's omniscience and such powers as could cure ailments with words.

Baba cured the neck and body pain of Laxmi Chand Jain of Delhi with semolina pudding.

KNEE-PAIN

Once Swami Sharan Anand was suffering from knee-pain. Baba asked him to touch the wooden pillar near the fire place with his knee and do 'pardakshna' around it. In the Dwarkamai, there is a three foot tall wooden pillar against which Baba used to lean while cooking. After doing as directed Swami Sharan Anand's knee- pain disappeared.

STOMACH ACHE

Datta Pant, a resident of Harda, had been suffering from stomachache for the last 14 years. When every medicine failed he came to Shirdi. Baba just looked at him with compassion and gave him 'udhi' as 'prasad'. Datta Pant's stomachache was cured immediately and it never occurred again.

Once Nana Sahib Chandorkar had an intense pain in the stomach and he could not rest or sleep during the day or night and all the injections and remedies given by the doctors having failed, he came to Baba with the complaint. Baba told him to eat 'burfi' with ghee and this wonder recipe gave him instant relief.

Kaka Mahajani's elder brother, Gangadhar Pant's stomach pain went immediately when Baba touched his stomach and assured him, " God will cure now."

EARACHE

A swami from Aladi could not sleep due to severe pain in his ears and though he was operated upon, they did not stop aching. He therefore went to Shirdi Sai Baba. When he was taking leave from Baba to go away from Shirdi, Shyama informed Baba of the Swami's pain. Baba said, "Allah achha karega" and blessed him. After that he was cured.

BACKACHE

Tarkhand's servant had acute pain in his lumbar region. Baba on hearing about his complaints prescribed that a particular type of leaves should be slightly heated, split into two and then be applied on the affected part. It gave instant relief when it was done.

SORE THROAT

A mere decision to visit Shirdi cured Mrs. Rangari of her inability to eat and drink on account of a sore throat.

ASTHMA

A six year old girl, suffering from chronic asthma, got cured in an unimaginable way through Baba's grace. Baba simply asked her to take a puff from His clay pipe.

In 1912, when Balaram Purandhar had gone to Shirdi, he went to Baba and started massaging Baba's legs. Baba who was then smoking His chillum gave it to him and asked him to smoke. Balaram who had never smoked earlier accepted His pipe, drew some puffs which he inhaled with tremendous difficulty and then returned it to Baba. For six years, Balaram had been suffering from chronic asthma and the moment he smoked Baba's chillum, the cure was effected.

STONES IN THE BLADDER

Dr. Khatte's two year old son, Vijay, was unable to take even milk and emitted particles of stone through the bladder. On coming to Shirdi, Vijay's mother asked him to have some of the food that Baba had begged and to their pleasant surprise Vijay had that food with his own hands. He was able to digest it and emission of bladder stones also stopped.

CHOLERA

Baba always advocated a course of treatment, which actually contradicted all known medical opinion. In fact such treatment, in common practice was sure to aggravate the ailment. Once Bapusahib Booty had an abnormal attack of cholera. He suffered severe pain in the stomach and severe thirst. Though he tried many medicines from Dr. Pillay and others, he got no relief. Then when he went to Baba for help, Baba prescribed an infusion of almonds, walnuts and pistachio---all boiled in sugared milk---a recipe which any doctor would consider simply mad, since it would aggravate rather than diminish the disease in the ordinary course of things. But since Booty had firm faith in Baba's words, that infusion was administered to him and strangely he was cured at once.

DYSENTRY

Once Mr. Booty, a millionaire devotee of Baba, suffered from dysentery. So much so that he could not go to the Dwarkamai. Baba sent for him and made him sit before him and said, " Now take care. You should not purge any more" and waving His index finger added, "The purging must stop." And it did stop. Mr. Booty was rid of the disease.

A week or two before Baba's samadhi Ramchander Samant had gone to Shirdi with the members of his family. While there, his two little sons had a severe attack of dysentery. In the normal course, the children would have been made to fast or given some light nutritional food or drinks but Baba prescribed that they be fed 'sheera'. They were given 'sheera' to eat and they were cured.

DIARRHOEA

Once Kaka Mahajani suffered from violent diarrhoea but he had to attend to Baba. So he kept a pot of water by his side and was often seen hurrying out to answer the call of nature. (In those days there were no latrines in the homes. People had to go out in the open to answer the call of nature.) They were sitting in the

Dwarkamai when Baba burst into a fit of anger. Every one ran away and Kaka Mahajani was about to do the same. But Baba forced him to sit there, picked up a handful of groundnuts from a bag left behind by one of those who had run away from there. He blew off the chaff and gave the clean nuts to Kaka Mahajani to eat. Baba too, ate some of the nuts, drank a little water from the pitcher and gave the rest to Kaka Mahajani to drink which he did fearing worse aggravation of the ailment. Something that should have aggravated the ailment, actually cured it!

By Baba's blessings Sushilamma Pillay who lived near Tirupati was blessed with a son in 1954. In 1955 the mother and the child suffered from fever and diarrhoea. Baba appeared in her dream and told her to wear a talisman which was lying in their cupboard. She did what she was directed and was cured. She started worshipping Baba with greater zeal. One day she found a metallic strip with a picture of Baba on it. She took it as a gift from Baba and put it around the child's neck. Her younger brother and her nephew started criticizing her for worshipping Baba, a Muslim. The same night her younger brother and her nephew suffered from sudden, unbearable pain in the stomach and diarrhoea. Sushilamma told Sh. Pillay that both of them had spoken of Baba as a Muslim and their illness might be a result of that. Sh. Pillay scolded them for their impertinence and told them to prostrate before Baba's picture in repentance and to promise that they would distribute some 'prasad' every Thursday if they were relieved of their sufferings. As soon as they obeyed Sh. Pillay's instructions their pain vanished.

EPILEPSY

Harish Chand Pitale's son suffered greatly from epilepsy and he tried several allopathic and aurvedic medicines and doctors. Having heard of Baba's greatness from Das Ganu, Pitale came to Shirdi in 1910 with his wife and children in search of a cure for his ailing son. He went to the Mosque and placed his ailing son at Baba's feet and prayed. Soon the boy began to roll. His mouth began to foam and, he started perspiring profusely. So much so the boy fell down senseless. The parents got frightened, for though their son used to get fits occasionally, none was as serious as the present one. Taking her son to be dead, his mother started weeping. However Baba told her, "Have patience. Do not weep. Take the boy to your lodgings. He will soon come to his senses." The Pitales did as they were directed by Baba. Soon after that the boy regained consciousness.

LEPROSY

When Baba cleaned his mouth and rinsed it some lepers and others suffering from various diseases approached Him and collected the water that He spat out and sprinkled it on their heads. Devotees said one leper was completely cured by it. Bhagoji's leprosy disappeared to a great extent after Sai Baba touched his body followed by the warmth of the Dwarkamai's 'dhooni'.

FEVER

Hari Sita Ram Dixit was at Shirdi. He was laid up with fever. Baba ordered him to go back to his house in Ville Parle, Mumbai. Baba said to him, "Go home. The fever will go in four days. Don't lie down on the bed but move about. Eat almonds, pistachio and 'sheera'." Then He asked Shyama to escort him. Every one at home was surprised when ailing Kaka Sahib reached home. There the doctors recommended complete bed rest but Kaka Sahib followed Baba's instructions. Every one thought that Kaka Sahib would die and started reviling him for pawning his senses to the absurdities of a mad 'faqir'. Exactly on the fourth day the temperature came down and showed normal.

Bhagoji Shinde, Raghu Shinde's younger brother, once suffered from high fever and his case was very critical. Baba went to his house and gave him medicines which He Himself had prepared. He also got the patient branded on his temples with red hot iron rods! The treatment worked and Bhagoji escaped death.

MALARIA

Bala Shimpi of Shirdi, a devotee of Baba, once suffered from malignant malaria. Though he tried all remedies he had no relief. So, he went to Baba and sought His help. Baba told him that he would be relieved if he fed a black dog with rice and curd in front of the Laxmi temple. Bala Shimpi was confused by the strange and unusual recipe prescribed by Baba. But he had full faith in Baba's words. To his surprise the rice and curd were ready when he reached home. He mixed them and brought the mixture to the Laxmi temple. To his greater surprise, he found a black dog coming to him, hungry and wagging its tail. Bala then placed that mixture of rice and curd before that dog, which it very happily ate and Bala's fever went from that very moment.

Radha Krishnamai was suffering from malaria. Baba stood in front of her house and asked for a ladder, which was brought in no time. Baba leaned the ladder against the wall of her house, climbed up and walked across the roof and climbed down again and got them to remove the ladder. Radhakrishnamai's malaria disappeared.

TYPHOID

Booty Sahib was once laid up with typhoid. He was staying in the Dixitwada. But he was too weak to go to the Dwarkamai for Baba's 'darshan'. Baba gave him 'udhi' and made him eat 'sheera'. In due course Booty recovered without any traditional medicine.

TUMOUR

When Mhalsapati' wife had gone to her parents, she developed a tumour but she did not inform her husband. It was a discovery when Baba told him about her tumour and promised to cure it. Soon he got a letter about the tumour and that it had been cured.

BOILS

Nana Sahib Chandorkar had a painful boil on one of his buttocks. The doctors finally decided that it should be removed surgically. Nana got panicky. A night before he was to be operated, Nana took Baba's photo and placed it beneath his pillow. The next day, fifteen minutes before the operation was to commence, Nana was lying face down on the bed. Suddenly a tile from the roof fell on Nana's buttocks. It made Nana groan but it burst the boil and expelled all the infection. So, the doctors felt there was no need to operate. After a few days Nana visited Sai Baba and the first words that He spoke were, "I removed Nana's boil with My fingers."

STRANGE AILMENT

Mrs. P Sulochna's father was suffering from a mysterious ailment. Even if he walked a furlong his legs would swell and swell so severely that he would only weep and roll on the ground. All medical treatment failed. One day, her mother told her father of the miraculous cures effected by Baba and suggested that he should seek Baba's blessings. "What shall I lose? If I am cured, it is well, otherwise nothing is lost." So saying, he at once, vowed that he would visit Shirdi if he was cured. Miraculously his pain vanished and he was able to walk any distance normally.

PARALYSIS

In 1911 a wealthy merchant came to Shirdi with his eight year old, paralyzed daughter who could neither walk nor stand. Baba asked them just to stay at Shirdi. On the third day she began to use her legs a little. On the eighth day she was able to walk!

Evil Spirits

The educated wife of a doctor had been ailing for some time. No doctor was able to diagnose or cure the disease. The lady would swoon, lock her jaws and remain unconscious for hours together. At last the doctor's father asked him to take his wife to Shirdi. "Just for a trial," he said. To satisfy his father, both of them went to Shirdi but the wife would not go near the Samadhi Mandir. She was dragged to the Samadhi Mandir with the help of a friend and made to prostrate before Baba. 'Udhi' and 'tirath' were thrust into her mouth. On the second day the spirit within started speaking, "I am a female Bhil ghost. I had pounced upon the lady and possessed her while she was returning from her parental home and standing under a tree. The holy water and the holy ash sprinkled over me have vanquished me. So I am leaving this lady forever and going away." Thus ended the lady's sickness and she returned home hale and hearty.

GENERAL SICKNESS

Mhalsapati's family was ill. A doctor prescribed medicines but Baba did not let them take the medicines. He treated them on His own and they got well without any traditional medicine.

SCORPION-BITE

Bapu Sahib Jog was stung by a scorpion. He complained to Baba about it. Baba cured it with a word of command. He said, "Go. The pain will go soon." And it did go in no time.

SNAKE-BITE

Shyama was bitten on his toe by a venomous snake. The poison began to spread in his body and cause unbearable pain. Shyama thought that his end was near. His friends wanted to take him to the temple where many were cured of snake-bites. But such was Shyama's faith in Baba that he ran to the Mosque to his beloved saviour. Strangely enough no sooner did he step into the Mosque Baba flared up and started shouting, "Oh vile priest do not climb up. Beware if you do. Go. Get out! Go down!" Poor Shyama was mortified and stood there dumb-founded. Then suddenly Baba's expression and voice changed and with his characteristic love and tenderness He said, "Do not fear. The Faqir is merciful and He will save you. Go and sit at home. Don't stir out. Have faith in Me and be fearless." To his great surprise, Shyama found that the pain had already vanished and he felt that the poison was withdrawing to the toe. He was further instructed not to lie down and sleep. Baba was, in fact, shouting and fretting at the poison in Shyama's blood and not at Shyama himself.

PILES

Once Shyama suffered from piles and when he told Baba of his ailment He asked him to go to the village grocer and get some articles. Baba prepared a decoction of the articles which Shyama had bought. Shyama got immediate relief when he drank that decoction. Then a couple of days later the piles troubled Shyama again and since he knew the recipe and how it was made, Shyama without intimating Baba brought the ingredients and prepared the decoction as Baba had done and drank it. But this time he was shocked to find his piles were aggravated and in utter fright he ran to Baba. Seeing Shyama Baba said, "Tell Me doctor, how is your stomach now?" Shyama felt ashamed and told Baba every thing. Baba pressed His hand, on Shyama's stomach and he was cured for good.

Baba's Udhi Cures

Baba fully knew that even the greatest of philosophers could not bear the slightest of toothaches and hence Baba's first concern was to remedy physical ailments like fits, fevers, cholera , plague, cancer, T B, and hundreds of ills and diseases known and unknown. He was sure, once that was done His devotees would surely and naturally search for relief from Him in their spiritual quest. "I give My men what they want because they should wish to have what I really want to give," Baba often used to say.

During His early days in Shirdi Baba was simply a Hakim for some years and people came to Him to get free medicines that He had prepared using herbs and leaves and other things that He had stacked. His services to the sick and the poor were free. His reputation as a village doctor was very high. As the patients began to swell in numbers, Baba stopped giving medicines and instead began giving them a pinch of 'udhi' from His sacred fire. He once told Kaka Dixit that His 'udhi' cured all ills both physical and mental and gave the receiver health and happiness. Baba's 'udhi' was, is and will surely always be not merely a symbol of the ephemeral nature of man's life on earth but means for securing for His devotees quick relief for all their physical, mental and spiritual ailments, complaints and other maladies. People were brought to Baba as a last chance or as a means of averting the coming perils. Baba's 'udhi' is a panacea for everything and every problem, past, present or future and its possession was/is an assurance to its holder against all dangers

TUBECULAR BONE ABSCESS

and mistakes. In other words, Baba's 'udhi' is not common place ash found in a temple but Baba Himself.

Dr. D. M. Mulky's nephew suffered from tubercular bone abscess, an incurable disease. Though he was treated by the best of surgeons available in 1915 or 1916, he was not cured. Luckily, his parents knew Kaka Dixit, who advised them to take the patient to Shirdi Sai Baba. The boy was made to sit in front of Baba who moved His hand over his diseased limbs. Within a few days of their stay in Shirdi, he was cured simply by applying Baba's 'udhi'.

HIP-JOINT CONSUMPTION

Sh. Keshawji after worshipping Baba with devotion had acquired certain powers. A boy who had been suffering from hip-joint consumption for four years was brought before him. The boy was carried by two men to attend the Thursday 'pooja'. Sh. Keshawji touched the boy's forehead and asked him to apply Baba's 'udhi' on the affected part and attend Thursday 'pooja' for seven weeks. At the end of seven weeks the boy became normal and led a normal married life.

Somnath Shankar Deshpande says that his brother was showing signs of incipient consumption. His father gave him 'udhi' and 'tirath' and he recovered.

PLAGUE

Nandram Marwadi visited Shirdi in 1911 at the time of the second great plague. Many were leaving the village in haste. One day, when he passed by the Maruti temple, some people seated there told him that his eyes were red with fever and he might be struck by plague. He wanted to quit the place and sought Baba's leave. Baba, however, dissuaded him. "As long as I am alive I will not let you die." He said and gave him 'udhi'. He stayed their and his fever vanished.

Bappaji, Shyama's younger brother, lived near Sawal Vihir on the Kopergaon Road. Once his wife was attacked by bubonic plague and two big buboes were seen on her groin, followed by very high fever. Bappa ran to Shyama in Shirdi and asked him to come to his house and help him in nursing his wife. Shyama then went to Baba, told Him the facts and sought His permission to go to Vihir and help his brother's wife who was quite seriously ill. Baba said to him, "Don't go now. It is too late in the night. Why worry about the buboes and fever? Send 'udhi'. She will be all right by His grace. But go in the morning and return immediately. Shyama sent Baba's 'udhi' through his brother, who returned home and applied 'udhi' on the frightful buboes and mixed some in water and gave it to her to drink. No sooner was the 'udhi' mixture swallowed than profuse perspiration set in on her entire body and the fever soon abated. The lady then slept and Bappaji was surprised to see his ailing wife recover so soon. When Shyama went to his brother's house, the next day he, too, was surprised to see her preparing tea near the hearth. Then he realized why Baba had prevented him from going the previous night and why Baba had said to him, "Return immediately."

Once a devotee of Baba wanted 'udhi' for his plague-stricken daughter who was away from him. Nana Chandorkar got word on the road near Thane railway station while he was going to Kalyan with his wife. At that time Nana too didn't have 'udhi' with him. So he took up some earth from the road, meditated and invoking Baba's aid applied the earth on his wife's forehead. The devotee himself saw this. When the devotee went to his daughter's place, he got to know that she had shown signs of improvement since the moment Nana had prayed and applied the earth on his wife's forehead.

Vinayak Daji Bhave says that in 1933 his son had plague and he recovered by the use of Baba's 'udhi' only.

STONES IN THE KIDNEY

An aged man of Harda was suffering from a stone in the bladder and the doctors had advised him to undergo an operation. Since he was old and weak and feared the knife and scissors that the doctors would use, he was not willing to go in for a surgical remedy. Then by chance there came the Imamdar of Harda, who was a Sai devotee and who had some 'udhi' of Baba. The 'udhi' was obtained from the Imamdar and mixed with water. It was given to the ailing man to drink. Within a matter of five minutes after 'udhi' was assimilated, the stones were flushed out with urine and the man was so miraculously relieved of the pain.

LEPROSY

Dr. Rane was a highly qualified doctor of Mumbai. He could not cure his wife of leprosy. In 1922 he took his wife to Shirdi. She applied 'udhi' and 'abhishake tirath' on the affected parts. In two years time she was completely cured of the disease and even the discolouration disappeared.

EPILEPSY

The daughter of an Irani man in Mumbai got fits of epilepsy every hour of the day and then she used to lose her power of speech. Her lungs would get frozen and shrunken. She would fall down senseless. Though every remedy was tried by the father there was no relief. A friend who knew Baba and the wonders of 'udhi', advised him to obtain 'udhi' from Kaka Dixit and see whether that could bring any relief to his young daughter. He secured the 'udhi' and gave it mixed with water to his daughter to drink and it worked. The convulsions which in the beginning happened every hour, came every seven hours and ultimately never troubled her again.

INSOMNIA OR SLEEPLESSNESS

In Bandra, a suburb of Mumbai, there was a man who suffered from sleeplessness. When he went to bed at night, his deceased father would appear in his dreams and scold him. So much so, it was not possible for him to get any sleep. Then a Sai devotee gave him 'udhi' and asked him to apply it on his forehead before he went to sleep and also to keep a packet of 'udhi' under his pillow every night. He followed the advice and found that the remedy worked. His deceased father never appeared in his dreams again.

NEURASTHENIA

Sh. Subhrao's daughter was suffering from neurasthenia from December 1939. She had lost her memory and fear dominated her life. In April, she was taken to Shirdi and given 'udhi' and 'tirath'. From then onward she began to have sound sleep. She started recovering and soon she became hale and hearty.

DUMBNESS / LOSS OF SPEECH

A little girl of Mumbai was run over by a car. She was saved but was injured. The hospital restored her health in a fortnight's time but her power of speech could not be restored. She had become dumb. A devotee gave her 'udhi' which he had received from the hands of Baba. She started speaking as soon as the first dose of 'udhi' was given to her.

BOILS

Mrs. X had boils on her legs. When medical treatment failed, her husband asked her to apply Baba's 'udhi' but there wasn't sufficient quantity of 'udhi' in the house. To their surprise, they received a packet of 'udhi' from Rahata, a miracle by itself. With that 'udhi' she was completely cured.

DELIVERY

Shridhar Narayan Kharkare's daughter was in the family way. In that condition they took her to a village where medical facilities were not available. At midnight it was found that the child had died inside the womb. The mother's condition became precarious. Sh. Kharkare took refuge in Baba's 'udhi'. He applied it on his daughter's forehead. Within an hour or so the dead child was born naturally. The child was dead, of course, but the mother was saved.

A lady from Mumbai used to suffer terrible pains at delivery time and so she would naturally be very frightened whenever she happened to conceive. She did not know what to do. A Sai devotee asked her husband to take her to Sai Baba for a painless delivery. So when that lady was pregnant next, the couple came to Shirdi and stayed there for a couple of months. They worshipped Baba daily and at last when it was time for the delivery there was as usual an obstruction in the passage from the womb and she began to suffer, giving up hopes of painless delivery. Womenfolk from the neighbouring houses in Shirdi came and invoking Baba's aid gave her His 'udhi' mixture to drink. Then in five minutes that lady had a safe and painless delivery. The child was born and its parents were happy.

FEVER

Tukaram Barku had been having fever for over two months. 'Udhi' was applied on his body and the very next day the fever ceased.

Once Vinayak Appaji Vaidya's three year old niece had high fever for days together. The fever went up to 105 degree. The end seemed to be near. Vinayak Appaji took refuge in Baba's 'udhi' and in three-four days the child became all right.

SWELLING

In 1932 Gopinath Joshi's three year old son had a huge swelling on the toe. The doctor wanted to amputate it. But 'udhi' effected the cure. There was no need for amputation.

SMALL POX

The same child had smallpox with high fever in the same year. Only 'udhi' and 'tirath' were given. The child recovered without any traditional medicine.

SCORPION BITE

Dr. B. G. Dass was running a clinic at Kanpur. As the clinic was located on the ground floor of their residence, Mrs. Dass used to visit it during her leisure hours. One day, a Muslim lady brought her eleven year old daughter who had been bitten by a scorpion. The Dass couple did not administer any medicine but applied 'udhi' on the affected part and gave the girl a mixture of water and 'udhi' to drink. The mother and the daughter were asked to remain in the clinic for some time. Even the doctor and his wife were surprised to see the girl fully cured of pain.

Narain Motiram Jain was a devotee of Baba. Once his friend was stung by a scorpion. It gave him immense, unbearable pain. He wanted to apply 'udhi' on the affected part of his friend's body but he found he had none. So he went home and stood before Baba's photo, said a fervent prayer for help and took a pinch of 'agarbatti' ash which was in front of Baba's photo and applied it on the site of pain and sting. To their surprise, he found that the ash worked like Baba's 'udhi'. The pain from the sting vanished at once.

CHOLERA

Mr. Sinha's neighbour was down with cholera. He gave him 'udhi' and the man got cured.

On 1-9-1932 Rasane had a very serious attack of cholera. Death seemed to be imminent. So much so his father asked him about his last wish. He replied that he wanted to go to Shirdi and be cremated there after his death. Then he took 'udhi' with coffee. Thereafter his fever ceased and he had no more motions. The cure was so sudden that it surprised all.

PNEUMONIA

Mr. Jadhav's son was down with pneumonia. It was the sixth day of his fever and the doctors had opined that the fever would run its course of nine days. When Mr. Jadav applied 'udhi' on the patient's forehead, the fever disappeared that very next day.

ITCH

Somnath Shankar Deshpnde's nephew had itch all over his head. His father gave him 'udhi' and 'tirath' and the itch was cured.

APPENDICITIS

Somnath Shankar Deshpande was suffering from pain in his side as though it was the commencement of appendicitis. So he wrote to his father. He came and applied 'udhi' on the affected part and from the very next day there was no more pain.

PARALYSIS

During his first visit to Baba, Moreshwar Pradhan stayed in Shirdi for eight days. On the third day of his visit Baba touched the limbs and said to him, "On this side of my body there is a terrible pain" and then added, "It will be all right within two to four days", No one understood the meaning of Baba's words or to whom they were said. After eight days He gave Pradhan leave to go from Shirdi. Chandorkar's son Babu who had accompanied Pradhan as it was his first visit to Shirdi, placed a plate beneath Baba's feet, washed them with water and took the water or 'tirath' home for use of other members of his family. Till that time only 'udhi' was allowed to be taken home and Baba's 'tirath' was consumed then and there. Pradhan also took his cue from his young friend and he too, collected some 'tirath' for use by his family members.

They had only third class tickets and under the rules they could catch only an ordinary passenger train. But at the platform there was a mail train going to Mumbai. Contrary to the rules they boarded the mail train and reached their homes some five or six hours earlier and those hours proved to be very crucial in Pradhan's life for it was only His grace that had brought him home early that day. As soon as Pradhan reached home he learnt his aged mother had a paralytic attack at Mumbai when Baba was saying in Shirdi that He was having pain in His sides. Doctors in Mumbai were summoned to attend to the lady and Mrs. Pradhan and others were thinking of informing Pradhan at Shirdi about the dreadful attack but Chandorkar who was then in Pradhan's house had remarked, "It would be needless and that everything would be safe for the lady as long as her son remained in Shirdi with Sai Baba and that Baba Himself would send him back to Bombay if and when Baba felt it necessary." On the night when Pradhan and his friends had departed from Shirdi for Mumbai the attendant doctors noticing there was constriction of her bowels, restlessness and high fever had pronounced her condition extremely critical and said that only if her bowels showed some movement, the situation would be hopeful and she could survive. It was on this very night that Moreshwar Pradhan had reached four or five hours earlier than the scheduled time of his passenger train. When he saw her state he administered Baba's 'udhi' and 'tirath'. At once his mother felt a bit sleepy and later her bowel also moved and her temperature fell. His mother soon recovered her health.

POLIO

Mr. M. K. Anandvankateshwarlu says that his unquestionable conviction in the existence of God came from his brother's recovery without any medical assistance. His third brother had lost the use of his left hand and left eye on account of polio which he had suffered from when he was three months old. Even at the age of ten years he could not stand. Owing to some financial problems, they could not provide him with any medical aid. Luckily he happened to meet Sh. Bhardwaj and Sh. Somnath Narain Maharaj. They heard the sad story of his brother and gave him Baba's 'udhi' to apply. They expected the 'Hanuman Chalisa' to be recited when the 'udhi' was applied. He sent this 'udhi' home along with the instructions. As they did not have a 'Hanuman Chalisa' they did not apply the 'udhi'. But strangely enough, from the fourth day of the sacred ash reaching their home his brother who was then unable to stand, started moving about with the help of a stick. Before he came to know of this miracle, one day early in the morning, he had a dream. Sai Baba was there surrounded by devotees of whom he was one. Pointing at him He told the others, "It is I that have saved this lame boy." He woke up at once wondering what this could mean and looked at Baba's picture. It occurred to him that Baba was refering to his brother.. After a few days he went home and to his pleasant surprise his brother was walking about with the help of a stick even though 'udhi' had not been applied on his body.

CHEST PAIN

One Dattopant of Harda town used to get shooting pain in the chest and all the remedies being exhausted he came to Shirdi. Sai Baba placed His hand on his head and blessed him with 'udhi' and the fourteen–year old disease left the man.

UNCONSCIOUSNESS

Once Laxman Govind Munge of Nasik had a guest and his guest's daughter staying with him. Suddenly his friend's daughter took ill and the case took a serious turn, as she lost consciousness and everybody in the house believed she wouldn't survive. Munge, an old devotee of Baba, took out Baba's photo and 'udhi' and placed the photo near her head and applied the 'udhi' on her face and body and the host and the guest both prayed for Baba's help. On the following morning the girl had regained her senses and within a few days she became completely normal.

EVIL SPIRITS

The house of a man was haunted and he had really become a playground for devils and evil spirits. Whenever he took off his clothes and hung them on the pegs, they would catch fire and start burning. Live worms and reptiles could be seen in the food. The man was naturally fed up with the misery that these happenings had brought on him. So, he changed his place of residence a couple of times and went for some 'mantras' and 'tantras' to check these acts of sorcery but there was no change and the evil spirits continued their game. He got himself transferred to another town but even there the same things continued unabated. Then learning of the kindness and powers of Baba he came to Shirdi and Baba applied 'udhi' on his forehead with His own hands and at once the magic spell left him for good.

UDHI FOR PROMOTION

A Faqir, who visited Appa Kulkarani's house, gave his wife a packet of 'udhi' and directed her to keep that packet in the house and worship it along with Baba's photo. Appa later examined the packet and found that it contained some petals of dried flowers, 'akshat' (yellow rice meant for pooja) and some 'udhi'. After some time Appa Kulkarani went to Shirdi and secured a strand of Baba's hair as His blessing and put the packet of 'udhi' in a talisman which he always wore on his arm and soon the power of 'udhi' began to manifest itself. Though he was an able and efficient officer earlier also, he got a paltry salary of fifty rupees per month but after he got Baba's 'udhi' and tied the talisman around his arm, he got a promotion and an increment. It was much more than his original salary.

22

Baba's Appearance to Protect

There are numerous incidents, which show that Baba has been taking different shapes to protect the lives of His devotees.

Baba as a 'Faqir'

In 1914, Ganpat Dhond Kadam was saved from a gang of Bhil robbers. He was proceeding to Shirdi with his family, when a gang of Bhil robbers boarded the running train and entered the compartment where he was reading a book of holy songs. Thinking that the Bhils were interested in listening to the songs he started reading them louder. The gang waited there for five minutes and then left the running train one by one. The wonderful part of the story is that Mr Kadam saw a faqir sitting in front of him as the gang boarded the running train and then as soon as they left the train the faqir disappeared. No one knew where. When Kadam reached Shirdi, Baba asked him, "Well, you have come safe and well–guarded?" Kadam at once realized that it was Baba who had appeared to him in the compartment, and as a result the gang left them all safe and sound.

Once S.B. Nachane's toddler was playing with older children. They were playing with crackers. The toddler's clothes caught fire. Since the mother's attention was somewhere else, a faqir pointed to the little child. The mother immediately ran towards her son and saved him from further injury. In the pell-mell the faqir disappeared. He was not there to receive thanks even.

Baba as an Old Man

Dass Ganu was a constable in the police department. Once he went on a pilgrimage without getting his leave sanctioned. His suspension was sure. When he realized this he prayed to Baba for help. Just then, there appeared an old man who told him that some boys had caught hold of a robber and that Ganu should go and arrest him. He rushed to the spot and arrested the culprit. When he reached the police station along with the robber and the booty, instead of being suspended he was promoted! How could the old man know that Ganu was a constable? How could innocent boys catch hold of a bloodthirsty robber? Why did the man himself not inform the police and get appreciation? It dawned upon him only then that it was Sai Baba who had come to help him.

Baba as a Fisherman

Once a poor clerk committed a serious blunder in his accounts and was afraid of dismissal. He was so frightened by this prospect that he decided to commit suicide. One day he kissed his child, wore old clothes and went out. His wife was aware of his mental condition. She knew it was no use trying to prevent him from going out. So she called him back, gave him 'udhi' and let him go. Then she sat before Baba's photo and prayed fervently to Him to save her husband's life.

Her husband who had left in the morning did not come back till late in the evening. How could he – as he had jumped into a secluded tank. A fisherman rescued him and threatened to hand him over to the police if he did not return home. He gave him a little money and left him at his house at 11 p.m. That very minute the fisherman disappeared.

Baba as a Vague Human Form

Sh. Manikshaw was a Sai devotee but he could not visit Shirdi for a long time. Once when he was on his way to Nagpur, he was sleeping in his reserved compartment. At 1.30 p.m. a vague human form appeared and said, "Don't proceed farther," and vanished. The train had reached Manmad. He got down. The next train for Nagpur was in the evening. The pilgrims proceeding to Shirdi suggested that he should join them and he did. By evening, he returned to Manmad and came to know that the earlier train by which he was travelling had met with a major accident and that many people had been wounded and killed. Baba had saved him from danger and had fulfilled his wish to visit Shirdi.

Baba as Baba

In 1927 a couple was returning to Mumbai after attending the Ramnaumi festival at Shirdi. At Thane the wife alighted to get a jug of water. Suddenly the train started and the woman fell down under the carriage. Everyone feared that the woman would have been crushed under the wheels. However, when the train halted and people reached the site of the accident, they found her standing there safe and sound. On being asked what had happened she said that Baba had pushed her to the edge of the platform and held her tight till the train left.

Mr K.D. Mattrey once visited Shirdi. In those days the Samadhi Mandir was under repair. His child, two years and a half, stood on the first floor. Suddenly the girl leaned forward and fell down from the terrace. Several devotees ran to her but the child stood up smiling and said, "As I fell down, the old man in that photo leaped up, held me in his hands and put me down."

23

Baba's Appearance to Help

Sai Baba was an evolved soul pervading the heart and soul of every creature. Though the Mosque at Shirdi was the seat of His physical living He appeared at will in different places and in different guises and looked after His men and their welfare in amazing ways.

Baba as a Bhil

Baba performed many miracles to instill faith in Chandorkar regarding His divinity. Chandorkar was going up a hill to a shrine. After a steep climb, he felt tired and thirsty but none of His companions or subordinates could get him a glass of water. He felt only Baba could help him. Just then he saw a Bhil. He told them that in the rock where they were sitting, there was water. They removed the slab and found drinking water to quench their thirst. At the time when Chandorkar was searching for water Baba in the Dwarkamai was saying, "Nana is thirsty. Should We not provide him a little water?" After some time when Chandorkar reached the Dwarkamai, Baba's query was, "Nana, you were thirsty. I gave you water. Did you drink it?"

Baba as a Peon

In 1928 Sh. S. B. Nachane lost his wife. He was so heart-broken that he became indifferent to his needs. He was going to Nasik to perform his wife's last rites. Baba assumed the form of a peon and sat on the seat opposite Nachane's seat and started conversing with him. He brought a blanket for him. He did it in no time so

Nachane asked Him if His house was near. He gave the address of an Arts College and said that his boss was away, so he was utilizing the opportunity to visit Nasik. He helped Nachane perform the last rites. He did whatever was required by Nachane. On coming back to Mumbai, Nachane went to the Arts College to thank the peon but there was no such peon in the Arts College. Baba Himself had come to give him company at a time when he was feeling lonely.

Baba as a Faqir

A cook stole Rs. 30,000 from his master. The master was perturbed as he could not find his servant. A Faqir appeared before him and asked him the cause of his depression. The Faqir recommended to him to forgo his favourite food till he got the money back and then go to Shirdi to see Sai Baba. So he stopped taking rice. Within a fortnight the cook appeared and returned the money.

Chhotubhai Palekar, an honorary magistrate, left Namwar to have 'darshan' of Baba Sidhnath. It was evening by the time they reached the river Narmada. The boatman refused to take them across the river. Mrs Palekar prayed to Sai Baba for help. Suddenly there appeared on the scene, a Faqir on a white horse. He, too wanted to cross the river but he also got the same reply. He said that he was going to get written permission from the authorities. The moment he turned His back the boatman agreed to take them across the river. The Palekars realized that the Faqir on the white horse was none other than Baba Himself.

Mrs. Chandrabai Borkar, an ardent devotee of Sai Baba, was at Shirdi and her husband was posted at Pandharpur. One day Baba said to her, "You had better go to Pandharpur and I will go with you. I need no conveyance to travel."

When Chandrabai reached Pandharpur her husband had left for Mumbai. She had very little money and two companions with her. She was sitting at the railway station and brooding. Suddenly a Faqir appeared before her and asked her why she was gloomy. She gave an evasive reply but was surprised when He told her that her husband was at Dhond and that she should go there at once. But she did not have enough money for the fare. The Faqir handed her three tickets to Dhond and went away before she could thank Him even. She then left for Dhond.

Meanwhile her husband, Mr. Borkar, was dozing on a bench at the railway station. A Faqir appeared before him and said, "Why do you neglect my mother? She is coming here by the next train." Then He gave him a slip bearing compartment number. Mr. Borkar got up wondering who the Faqir could be. Just then a train arrived and Chandrabai stepped down from the railway carriage of the same number as was mentioned on the slip given by the Faqir. Borkar received her and told her of his strange experience and asked her to show him a picture of Sai Baba. It was the same Faqir who had appeared before him.

Baba as a Friend

Once a Sai devotee came to seek financial aid for the marriage of his daughter. Baba simply said, "God will help." The devotee was very disappointed. When he reached his home he was surprised to see that his wife had made every arrangement. She told him that a friend of his had returned the money he might have lent him. But he knew he was never rich enough to lend money. It was Sai Baba who had come to him in the form of a friend.

Baba as a Fellow Passenger

Govind Ram Samant came to Shirdi. He had only five rupees. He gave one rupee as 'dakshina' and kept four rupees for the return journey. Baba demanded one rupee more. He had to part with it reluctantly. On receiving the second rupee Baba said to him, "You have given two rupees to this Faqir, Ganu Maharaj will help you." He could not understand what Baba meant by these words. He started for Kopergaon with a palpitating heart as he didn't have sufficient money to buy the ticket. When he was waiting for the tonga there came a Gujrati who gave him a lift. Then the man bought tickets for both of them. Govind Ram Samant was thankful to him for the timely help. He took his name and address as he wanted to return the money spent on the fare. The next day when he went there he found that it was a Muslim colony and no one by that name lived there. Then he realized that by Ganu Maharaj Baba meant Ganpati. Baba had come to him as Ganu Marwadi.

Baba as an Old Man

Once Chandorkar wanted to visit the Ganpati Mandir. It was night and he got lost in the jungle. He desperately needed a guide. Suddenly he saw an old man at a distance. He tried to come abreast of him to enquire the way but the old man moved faster. Chandorkar, too, had to double his speed. Suddenly the old man disappeared and Chandorkar realized he was near the Ganpati temple.

An advocate from Boribandar once started for Shirdi with Rs. 100 in his pocket. Unfortunately his pocket was picked and he lost the money and his railway ticket. Later when the ticket examiner came, he did not relent even after hearing about the theft. Just then an old gentleman gave the lawyer a ticket and said that his man had not joined him as promised. He introduced himself as a devotee of Sai Baba and bore all the advocate's expenses. At Shirdi the old man presented him with a copy of a book on Sai Baba and also gave him his address in Mumbai. Later when he opened the book the advocate found Rs. 100 in it. When he returned home he found his purse before Baba's picture in his family shrine!. He went to Mumbai but the old man's address could not be traced. The advocate kept the money he had found in the book in his shrine for worship. Thereafter his financial condition improved considerably.

Baba as a Bullock-cart Driver

In the rainy season of 1948 a batch of Hyderabadi devotees left for Shirdi. There was no direct bus service from Kopergaon to Shirdi so the travellers had to cross the Godawari by ferry. The cart driver who had brought them up to the bank of the river offered to take them across in his bullock-cart. The river was already in spate and as it started raining, it became furious. The cart-driver lost control. The devotees knew for certain that they were going to meet a watery grave. So they started chanting Sai Baba's name. Suddenly from nowhere a middle-aged man appeared in front of the bullock-cart and assumed control of steering the cart of his own sweet will. The stranger piloted the cart towards the other shore. On reaching the other shore the party rejoiced with shouts of "Sai Baba ki jai". The group leader took out a ten-rupee note to give to the stranger. But lo! The stranger was not there.

Baba as a Villager

One day Mankar wished to go to Dadar, Mumbai. There was a great rush and there seemed to be little hope of getting a ticket in time. Suddenly, a villager clothed only in a loin cloth and wrapped in a coarse woollen blanket approached him and enquired about his destination and handed him a ticket to Dadar. He said that as he himself dropped his intended journey to Dadar, he was willing to give the ticket to him. Before Mankar could pay for it, the man disappeared in the crowd and could not be traced any where.

One evening Mr. Pathak, the former in-charge of the Sai Baba Sansthan, Shirdi, received an urgent message that 600 devotees were visiting Shirdi that night. He needed Rs. 1200 to make arrangements for them. But by that time the day's collection of the Samsthan had already been deposited in the treasury. He sat in his office worrying about how to manage. Two villagers entered his office and said that they wanted to pay six hundred rupees to the office for feeding the devotees. Mr. Pathak told them to see him the next morning as the office was closed and no payments could be accepted. They said that they were in a hurry and requested him to accept their money and make arrangements for the next day. Mr. Pathak accepted it. One of them mentioned his name as Shirdikar that is a resident of Shirdi). After that they went away. Then Mr. Pathak remembered that he had not thanked them for their timely contribution and asked the peon to call them back but they were not to be found anywhere.

Three days later Dr. Gowankar, an old devotee of Baba, came from Mumbai and said to Mr. Pathak, " Three days ago I had a dream in which I saw Baba and Abdul Baba enter your office and give you money."

Baba as an Acquaintance

Dr. Rustam was a homeopath in Shirdi. He owed three hundred rupees to some one in Bombay. The doctor went to Bombay and handed over a cheque for three hundred rupees to the person concerned. But when he came back to Shirdi, to his dismay, he found that he did not have enough money in his bank account. He was afraid that the cheque would be dishonoured. He appealed to Baba for help. A couple of days later a casual acquaintance came to him with a packet containing three hundred rupees to be kept with him for three months. Rustamji asked him if he could use the amount during that period. The visitor had no objection as long as he got the amount back after three months. At the end of three months Dr Rustam waited for the man to come back and claim his money but the man did not turn up. One day, Rustamji saw him and tried to hand over the amount to him but the man refused to accept the money. He said he had never given any money to Rustamji.

Mr. H. S. Dixit was one of the most ardent devotees of Sai Baba since 1910. In 1923 he was in trouble. He had to repay a debt of Rs. 30,000. He felt if Baba were alive He would have solved his problem. Suddenly, there appeared a young man who told him that he was Mr. Dixit's acquaintance's son. He had brought a sum of thirty thousand rupees to keep in Mr. Dixit's custody. Mr. Dixit told him of the situation he was in and that he would not be able to repay the amount soon. The young man had no objection as he had full faith in Mr. Dixit's integrity.

Baba as a Young Man

Mr. R S Chitnis of Delhi reached Shirdi at noon. He wanted to have a wash before he went to the Samadhi Mandir for 'darshan' but there was not a drop of water in any of the taps. Mr. Chitnis was nonplused. A well-dressed young man with a piece of cloth around his head came towards him and took him to a bathroom where there was sufficient water. Mr. Chitnis took a bath and went for the 'darshan' but he found himself at the end of a serpentine queue. Once again the same stranger appeared and took him to Baba's idol. Mr. Chitnis was assailed with fear that people would object to his breaking the queue but no one raised even an eyebrow in protest. After the 'pooja' when he came out, he wanted to thank the stranger but he had disappeared.

When he reached his car where other members of his family were sitting, all of them said in a chorus that there was no water and hence they could not bathe. Mr. Chitnis wanted to take them to the bathroom where he had taken a bath. He could not find that bathroom. Everybody said that for an hour and a half there was no water in any of the bathrooms. Everyone wondered who had arranged water for Mr. Chitnis.

Baba as a Stranger

In 1943 when Kasavaya visited Shirdi, he had a wish to go to Pandharpur and he proceeded on his journey. A stranger met him and accompanied him. He even paid for the conveyance. After making all the necessary arrangements he said to Shri Kasavaya, "Whenever you think of me I shall come to you" and then he disappeared.

Baba as a Constable

Bhaskar Sadashiv Satam joined police force in 1911. In February 1940 he was suspended. Ten years earlier his friend had suggested to him that he should go to Shirdi. Now he decided to visit Shirdi and pray to Baba. When he came back to Mumbai a constable told him that he had been reinstated and posted to the Lemington Road Police Station. Satam knew it for certain that no such order could have been passed by that time because he had appealed against the dismissal on 28-4-1940. Ultimately when the appeal was heard the order passed was, "Reinstated and posted to Lemington Road

Police Station." Baba had given the verdict two months earlier through the constable.

Baba as a Sadhu and a Peon

Once two visitors came to Shirdi. In their presence Baba started narrating His experiences. He said once when he was living in a palace some one stole 30,000 rupees from him. It was a very big amount in those days. He was depressed. Then some sadhu told him to forgo his favourite food till he got his money. He did as he was directed. Within a few days the thief, his own cook, came back and returned the money. Then he wanted to thank the Faqir. So, he went to the captain of the ship but there was no seat. Then there appeared on the scene a peon who told him that he was waiting for him. Thus through the him he got the seat and travelled. Shyama and others sitting in the Dwarkamai were sure that Baba had never gone beyond Rahata and Neemgaon. How could He travel by steamer? Moreover He never had a huge amount of money. One of the visitors remarked that it was his story that Baba was narrating.

24

Invisible Appearance

Baba took many forms to help and protect His devotees if they were in trouble. But there are instances when He did not take any physical form but still helped them.

Once Kashi Ram Shimpi, a weaver, was attacked by robbers in the jungle. As his life was in danger he invoked Sai Baba's help. Somehow, he felt that he could face the robbers on his own. He snatched a sword from one of the robbers and killed two others though he had never held a sword in his hand and obviously did not know how to use it. Another robber attacked Kashi Ram with an axe and he became unconscious. Taking him to be dead, the robbers fled from the scene. Kashi Ram lay there bleeding. When he regained consciousness he refused to go to any hospital, so the passersby brought him to the Dwarkamai. Devotees confirmed that at the time when Kashi Ram was struggling with the robbers, Baba was abusing and waving his sataka in the direction of Kashi Ram. This was a method used by Baba to save his devotees from trouble.

In 1926, Mrs Manager and her family left for Shirdi. At that time she was six months pregnant. Unfortunately, the child within the womb died and for days she did not deliver. Mrs Manager started turning blue as there was blood poisoning. Medicines were brought from Ahamednagar but they were of no use. 'Udhi' and tirath were given. Even though she was unconscious, Mrs Manager started giving instructions which were followed. Thus Baba saved His devotee's life!

25

Dream to Communicate

*I*f Baba wanted to say something to somebody He did not say it openly. He made use of a dream to say it. Dreams, a very powerful means of communication, were used by Baba during His life time and are being used even now.

Abdul Sultan popularly known as Abdul Baba was just twenty when he came to Shirdi in 1889 or 1890. His parents who were very poor had given him into the care of a faqir named Amirudeen. It is said that Baba came in Amirudeen's dream and asked him to send Abdul to His Mosque in Shirdi. At the same time He gave him two mangoes. When he woke up he found the two mangoes on his bed. He realized it was not just a dream but a vision. So he directed Abdul to go to Shirdi. Baba welcomed him with the words, "My crow has come."

Sai Baba appeared to a lady in her dream. He was standing at her door and begging for 'khichdi'. Later the couple went to Shirdi and stayed there for two months. The lady wanted to offer 'khichdi' to Baba as she thought that he wanted it from her. On the seventeenth day of her visit, she prepared it and went to offer it. Baba had already sat down to have lunch and the curtain had been lowered. She was hesitant to enter. Somehow she made bold and entered. Baba at that time was saying that He wanted to eat 'khichdi' first but the devotees did not have it. When the lady offered it, Baba took it and ate it eagerly. She understood then that the dream she had at home was not just a dream but a vision.

One Christian officer, Joseph of Mumbai having failed to get any clue about the culprits in a criminal case, prayed to Baba to help him. Baba appearred in his dream and gave him the necessary instructions for investigation. By following Baba's instructions, Joseph was able to nab the culprits.

Baba helped Mr. Tendulkar in getting a fairly good pension. He had spent a major part of his life in serving a particular company but with the passage of time he started having epileptic fits and his vision, too, dimmed. So he applied for pension, which as a rule, could be fixed at seventy-five rupees, that is half of the total salary. Mrs. Tendulkar was upset as with this meager amount as she felt she would not be able to manage the whole household. She prayed to Baba who appeared in her dream and said, "I have a mind to fix up your pension at hundred rupees. Will that satisfy you?" A fortnight after the dream the company considered Tendulkar's application and going beyond the usual rule, fixed his pension at hundred and ten rupees.

One evening, Baba asked Kaka Dixit to go to Rahata and fetch Khushal Chand as He had not seen him for a long time. When Dixit went there in a tonga to fetch Khushal Chand, he was already getting ready to come to Shirdi. Khushal Chand told Dixit that Baba had appeared in his dream in the afternoon and asked him to come to Shirdi.

Nagamma suffered from intense poverty. In spite of her poverty, she attended Sai poojan every Thursday, without fail. One night, a "faqir" gave her money in her dream. Within a week of dreaming this, her son got employment. Her sufferings were at an end.

When the family pandit of Mr. and Mrs. Pradhan attributed their son's illness to the wrath of the Hindu gods, Baba appeared in his dream and told him He is Dattatrey and not a Muslim faqir.

A gang of four trespassed into lawyer, Vaman Chintamani's house by boring a hole in the wall. They removed a small trunk containing important papers and two hundred rupees. When they were removing a big trunk containing ten thousand rupees, silver vessels and gold jewellery, Chintamani's sister-in-law woke up and seeing the intruders called out, "Thief! Thief! Thief!" But the

Dream to Communicate

lawyer was too fast asleep to wake up. So Baba appeared in his dream and said, "Get up! Get up! You are being robbed." At once the lawyer woke up frightened and ran with a cudgel in his hand shouting, "Thief! Thief!" The thieves, took fright left the house through the hole they had made. So the lawyer was saved. Even the small trunk, which they had taken out was left behind in fright. It was brought to the lawyer by the owner of that field.

In 1917, an examinee of a medical course saw a dream in which Baba told him, " I am having very severe pain in my stomach. Find out a suitable medicine and give it to Me." Naturally he tried to find out the answer to that question. The next day he found a similar question in the question paper and he was fully prepared for it.

In 1917, Hemadpant was in Bandra, Mumbai. Baba appeared in his dream as a well-dressed 'sanyasi', woke him up and told him that He was going to be their guest that day. So he made preparations but wondered how Baba could come all the way to Bandra. At lunch time, two Muslims came with a packet. When the packet was opened, it was a portrait of Baba. Hemadpant placed the portrait on the central seat meant for the chief guest, did 'pooja' and offered 'navaidya'.

Baba appeared simultaneously in the dreams of Bapusahib Booty and Shyama and clearly ordered them to build a 'wada' with a temple in it. The Samadhi Mandir is the result of that dream.

Sai Baba is as alive today as He was while in flesh. Baba took 'samadhi' on 15th October 1918. Mrs Pradhan of Mumbai records her experience on the night of 15th-16th. She says, "That night I saw His body in a dying condition in my dream and I said, "Baba is dying." Immediately Baba replied "People don't talk of saints as dying but of taking samadhi." His body was still. People were mourning. I felt sad. I woke up at 12:30 midnight. In the morning we got a postcard from Anna Chinchinikar intimating us that Baba passed away at 3 p.m. on the holy Dusehra ie 15-10-1918. On the same night Mrs. Pradhan's sister-in-law also saw Baba in her dream. He asked her to bring 'pitamber' (yellow cloth) to be placed on the samadhi.

Baba took 'samadhi' on the Tuesday on 15-10-1918. On Wednesday morning Baba appeared to Laxman Mama Joshi in his dream and drawing him aside by the hand, said, "Get up soon. Bapu Sahib Jog thinks I am dead and he won't come. You do the worship and the kakad arati." On the same night, Baba appeared to Das Ganu at Pandharpur and said, "The Masjidmai has collapsed. So I have left the place. I came to inform you here. Go there quickly and cover Me with bakul flowers." So the information that Das Ganu got through a letter from Shirdi only confirmed the truth of Baba's statement.

On 27-10-1918 Baba appeared in Kaka Mahajani's dream and said, "You are still sleeping? Get up and worship Me. Today is the thirteenth day celebration after My samadhi." Kaka Mahajani woke up and found it so. He made arrangement at once for 'brahm bhoj' and invited Kaka Dixit, Pradhan and Dabholkar for lunch. All of them sang 'bhajans' the whole day.

At the mahasmadhi of Baba there was a dispute between the Hindus and the Muslims. The Muslims wanted to erect a tomb at the place which Baba had pointed out to Mhalsapati in 1886 in case He did not revive from the trance after three days. The Hindus wanted to make His samadhi in the Bootywada. At last Baba had to appear in the dream of a responsible Muslim and tell him that He wanted to rest in the Bootywada as He Himself had inspired Mr. Booty to construct the wada where He used to have a lawn. In the morning the man conveyed the dream and the issue was settled very amicably. The Bootywada became the Samadhi Mandir.

Abdulla Jaan was a young Muslim Pathan of Peshawar. As he had no one in the world, he was leading a nomadic life. He wanted to visit Mecca but he had no money. Somebody told him that in Shirdi there was a Baba who was very liberal and he might help him financially. So in 1913 he reached Shirdi and till the year of Baba's samadhi his dream to visit Mecca remained unfulfilled. After Baba's samadhi he left Shirdi and reached the tomb of Akum Baba, the direct descendant of prophet Mohammad. He prayed to Akum Baba to help him visit Mecca. In the dream he saw Sai

Baba, and not Akum Baba. He felt that was an assurance from Sai Baba that He still cared for him.

After Baba's samadhi Shyama kept a packet of 'udhi' in his shrine. Once when he was at Mumbai, Baba appeared in his dream and said, "The packet of 'udhi' which I had given you is now lying in the dustbin by the side of your house. Go home at once and restore it." Shyama rushed home and looked for the packet in the shrine but it was not there. As the house was being repaired, all the articles in the house had been removed and in that process the packet was misplaced. Shyama searched for it outside and it was there in the dustbin!

Once Mr. Mehrotra, an agent of a bank, was suspended. He visited Shirdi and prayed to Baba for help. Baba appeared in his dream and gave him in writing, "You shall be reappointed as an agent. Do not fear." Shortly after that he was reappointed.

Mr. Shinde's neighbour was down with some ailment and he cured him with the medicine recommended by Baba in his dream. Then that man gave him a shawl which he wanted to present to Baba. In the meanwhile, Baba had taken samadhi. Once again Baba appeared in his dream and asked him to sell the shawl and with a part of the money buy rice and distribute it among the needy and with the rest of the money he could start his business. He did as he was directed and in no time the penniless man became a big business man.

Shantaram Balwant Nachane was a Sai devotee since 1912. In 1921 he became a widower. His parents were arranging for his second marriage. There were two proposals – one from a rich family and the other from a poor girl. The man was naturally attracted towards the rich girl but Baba knew his interests best. He appeared in his mother's dream and showed her the poor girl was suitable for her son. And she did prove a suitable life partner for him.

In 1923, a certain gentleman came to see Sh. M. B. Chauhan's sister for marriage and agreed to marry her. A formal letter of acceptance was to follow in a week's time. But for six months there was no reply. Mr. Chauhan's mother got desperate. One night she had a big fight with Baba. She challenged Baba to get her a reply by the next day. At night Baba appeared in her dream and asked her not to be angry as by 9a.m. she would get the response. When she got up in the morning, she forgot about the dream. But at 9a.m. when she was serving breakfast, the postman came with the letter of acceptance.

In 1924, a marriage agreement took place between Mr. Shirian, an ardent devotee of Baba and his friend. It was that his friend's son would marry his daughter after completing his education. After completing his education the boy's market value went up and hence there were many rich seekers. Mr. Shirian was poor by that standard. He felt frustrated and appealed to Baba, who appeared in his dream and told him that in two years time the same boy would marry his daughter. During those two years no marriage proposal of that boy materialized and he realized that it was because they had gone back on their commitment to Mr. Shirian. So at the end of two years the marrige took place as fixed by Baba.

In 1932, Appaji was in trouble. He owed three hundred and fifty rupees to one Marwadi of Shirdi who threatened to get him arrested. Appaji turned to Sai Baba for help. Baba appeared in his dream and instructed him to read certain stanzas of the Geeta and with that his debt would be cleared. Appaji was frightened when the creditor came to his office. He asked Appaji to build a house for him and on its completion he would write off his debt. Appaji was able to finish that in one month and so he was free from debt.

In 1940, in a dream Sh. Ram Lal was directed by Baba to build His temple on the land, which belonged to a labourer named Richivadu. This man had never heard of Sai Baba. But Baba appeared in his dream twice and directed him to give the land to Ram Lal for the construction of a temple. Richivadu told Ram Lal about his dream. The latter showed him the portrait of Baba, which he recognized to be of the one who was coming in his dreams. So he handed over the land and with the help of the community and Richivadu's labour, a 10 by 8 feet temple was ready within 4 weeks.

Inside the Chavadi there is a large portrait of Baba, which was painted by Abrahim from Navsari in Gujrat after Baba had given him 'darshan' in a dream in 1953. Abrahim was only 18 years old at that time.

There is an interesting story about the statue of Baba that was installed in the Samadhi Mandir thirty six years after His mahasamadhi. Some white marble arrived from Italy. Nobody knew anything about the sender or the receiver. In the absence of a claimant, the dockyard auctioned it and the purchaser offered it to the Shirdi Sansthan. Impressed by the quality of the marble they wanted to use it for Baba's idol and gave the contract to Balaji Vasant Talim, a sculptor from Bombay. The latter had only one black and white photo of Baba as his model and was struggling to get the likeness. One night Baba came to him in a dream, remarked on his difficulties and then showed him His face from various angles, encouraging him to study it thoroughly and remember it well. This gave Talim the fillip he needed and after that the work flowed easily and the result exceeded all expectations.

Two girls and a boy were born to Dattatrey Rasane but they all expired within few months of their birth. He was grieving at the demise of his son and in that state of depression he prayed to Baba thus, "Instead of giving me many babies that die quickly give me at least one child who will live long." After that Baba appeared in his dream. The dead child was on His lap and He said, "I took away this child because he was born in 'mool nakshtra' (a constellation of stars that is not conducive for the parents especially for the father). Don't worry. I'll give you a good child." In the morning when he looked up his dead child's horoscope it was a fact that he was born in that inauspicious constellation of stars. Moreover Rasane had a son within eighteen months of that dream.

Gangadhar Vishnu was five when his father expired and their land was usurped by some one. The other party too was a devotee of Sai Baba. In 1901, when he was 16 both the parties came to Baba for the settlement of the dispute. Baba asked the other party to hand over the land to the actual owner but the man did not. On

27-6-1935 Gangadhar Vishnu Khirsagar had a dream. He saw Baba standing before him and saying, "Today your house is decreed to you. Why are you sleeping?" Four days later, he got a letter from his brother that they had won the case about their land. The date of the decision coincided with the date of his dream.

Dattatrey Vithal Vaidya says that in 1935 his father was worried about his sister's marriage. He prayed to Baba for help. One night he had a dream. In that dream he was told by Baba that a letter from Pandharpur side would come and that would settle the matter and he need not be anxious. Within 15 days of that dream there came a proposal from Pandharpur and the marriage was settled and celebrated.

In 1933 Vinayak Appaji Vaidya had a dream, in which he gave one rupee to Baba. But Baba returned the rupee with the words, "Take as much as you want." Within one month of that dream he got a promotion unexpectedly.

A little before Sh. Pillay retired from service, the family was at a village called Madipadu. Their son had finished his post graduation with distinction. They wished that their son should get employment. So he stayed with their relations at Tummalgunta, trying for a job. In due course he got an interview call for a post in the Sh. Venkteshwara University, Tirupati. But he felt it was not worthwhile attending it as many applicants there would be with recommendations from big-wigs. He had no such help. But, still he attended it. Then he came to Madipadu. On 24-8-19976, Baba appeared to Smt. Sushhilamma in a dream and said, "Your son has got an appointment and the posting orders have been sent to Tummalgunta. Get them from there and let him join service." She woke up and told her husband about the dream. He brushed it aside as a mere projection of her own wishful thinking. Baba again told her the same thing the second day. She told her son about it but he too did not pay heed to it. Again on the third day Baba appeared in her dream and said, "Do not mind what your husband says. Get the appointment orders from Tummalgunta and

Dream to Communicate 171

send your son to take charge. Do not delay." In the meanwhile the relatives with whom their son had been staying left for a vacation for a month. The posting orders had been thrown into the locked house. But for Baba's timely invention the boy would have lost the opportunity to join service.

One Madhushah, a faqir, once came to Shirdi and asked Baba to give him Rs. 700 to fulfil some urgent need and cried and cried lika a child to get that amount from Baba. So Baba asked Bapusahib Jog to give him the amount he wanted. Jog brought the amount and placed it – all in silver coins – before Baba. Baba told two boys Gulab and Laxman Bala Shimpi to hand over the sum to the faqir who was seated before Baba. But while giving the money the boys played mischief. They misappropriated two hundred rupees and gave only five hundred rupees. He cried and cried that he was given two hundred rupees less but Baba did not listen to him. So the faqir got His 'udhi' and went from there on foot. When the faqir was nearing Neemgaon, a tonga came up in front of him and Irrus Shah, a Parsi gentleman alighted from the tonga and came to the faqir, gave him the food he carried and delivered Rs. 200 and then asked, "Are you now content?" Later Irrus Shah came to Shirdi, went to the house of Tatya Patil and narrated to him and others his own wonderful story. He had a dream in which Baba appeared to him and told him to go by tonga to Shirdi. He dreamed that on his way, near Neemgaon he would see a faqir who would be wearing a tiger skin on his body and he (Iris Shah) should give him food for the faqir would be hungry. Baba also asked him to give him Rs. 200, the money he needed. Irrus Shah said, so he had gone in a tonga with food and money and given them to the unknown faqir.

Yashwant Galwankar went to Baba in 1911 because his father-in-law (Hemadpant, the writer of Sai Satchrit) and others went to Him and not out of any desire to obtain any temporal or spiritual benefits. After that he went to Shirdi seven more times as his interest in Baba gradually increased. Once Baba appeared to Galwankar in his dream and demanded two rupees as His dakshina

Galwankar sent it the next day to Baba by money order. He was advised by Baba to behave with probity and integrity in his dealings and to be chaste with women in his dream. This advice Galwankar followed later in life with care and zeal.

M. B. Rege was a devotee of Vishnu. He was so much in love with Vishnu that he wanted to attain the height attained by Dhruva. His devotion bore fruit. He had three dreams in quick succession. In the third dream he saw Vishnu with another personality. Pointing to Him, Vishnu said to Rege, "This Sai Baba of Shirdi is your Guru. You must resort to Him." At that time M. B. Rege was a student. He could not go to Shirdi to verify Vishnu's statement. As soon as he grew up and became financially independent he went to Shirdi in search of his guru and found Him in Sai Baba.

When Captain Hate was staying in Bikaner, Baba appeared in his dream and the captain offered Him 'walpapadi', a vegetable. The captain thought that in this dream Baba actually demanded 'walpapadi' from him. So he wrote to a friend in Mumbai, sent him twelve rupees and requested him to go to Shirdi and on his behalf offer 'walpapadi' and other articles to Baba. He was to offer the rest of the money as "dakshina." The man went to Shirdi and with great difficulty purchased the required articles and offered them to Baba. The next day Nana Sahib Nimonkar got the vegetable made and offered it as 'navaidya'. All were surprised during the meal. Baba ate only the 'walpapadi' without touching rice and other items of food in the 'navaidya' plate. The message that Captain Hate received was the message that Baba wanted to convey.

Once a sick rich man came to Shirdi. As there were only ladies accompanying the sick man, they sent Prof. Narke to Baba to get them 'udhi'. So Narke went to Baba and asked for His 'udhi'. Baba, however, told him the man would be better quitting the earth, "What can the 'udhi' do? Anyway, take the 'udhi' and give it to him as it is wanted by them," Baba told Narke. So the professor took Baba's 'udhi' and gave it to the ladies, without, of course, disclosing to any one what Baba had said. The man's condition grew worse and Shyama went to Baba and told Him of the man's imminent end, "How can he die? In the morning he will come to life", said Baba. They hoped that the man would not quit the earth. But the man died. For hours together they kept on waiting for the man to get up from his eternal sleep. But that did not happen. They were much disappointed. They stopped visiting Shirdi. Then one day a close relative of the deceased man saw Baba in a dream with the head of the deceased mounted on His head. Then Baba, showed him his lungs which were rotten and stinking and said to him, "I saved him from the torture of this." After that his relatives renewed their visits to Baba as the misunderstanding had been cleared.

Martand, a poor tailor of Shirdi, was ill and bed-ridden. There was no one at home to look after him. So Baba appeared in his dream and asked him to go to Nana Sahib Dengle at Neemgaon and futher told him that he would be treated well by Nana Sahib and would soon recover. Then the sick Martand Darji somehow managed to go to Neemgaon where as soon as Nana Sahib Dengle saw him, he said, "You are most welcome. Stay here and make this your home. Do not worry. Last night Baba appeared in my dream and ordered me to render medical treatment to you." Martand was overcome by Baba's love for someone as poor as him. He stayed in Neemgaon, recovered and then returned to Shirdi.

26

Dream to Warn

Shri R.B. Purandhare was so much attached to Baba that he wanted to be near him all the time, ignoring his official duties. On one occasion he was anxious to go to Shirdi but at night, Baba appeared in his dream and said, "Beware if you come. I will hit you. Why should you come so often? I am not away from you. I am with you. Don't play the fool." As he was wondering why Baba had asked him not to come to Shirdi, there was a strike in his office and he realized that if he had left Mumbai he would have been considered as supporting the strike and had gone to Shirdi to hide the fact.

Mrs and Mr Vinayak Appaji Vaidya were ardent devotees of Baba. In 1923, Baba appeared in Mrs Vaidya's dream and forewarned her about a case to be filed against her husband, but at the same time assured her not to worry as He was there to look after them.

One night, Baba appeared in the dream of Sulochna's father, showed him a native of their village and said, "This man is about to enter your house to commit theft. Take care." Her father, at once, got up, secured all the doors of the house and slept peacefully. The next morning the person shown by Baba in the dream happened to meet him. Just to verify his dream, Sulochna's father accosted him, "How is it you were moving about in our street at night?" pretending to have actually seen him. The man was stunned and asked, "How did you know?" "Our cow was not to be seen and I came out in search of it," said her father. The manner of his response showed that he had ill intentions.

In 1932 Sh. M.V. Sahastrabudh, a civil engineer, was digging up the earth and laying drainage pipes with a large number of workmen. One afternoon, as he was napping under a tree, he was roused from his sleep. Baba said, "Get up. A man is being buried owing to the slipping of the earth. Go and remove him at once." He woke up, called his coolies and cycled up to the place of the accident, which was two miles away. He found that two sides of the trench had come down and buried twenty men. They dug up the earth. All, except one, were rescued with little injury. This one man was seriously hurt. He was bleeding from the nose and mouth, and his eyes were bulging out. He wanted to be taken home. However, as soon as he reached there, he died. But for Baba's rousing the civil engineer this man would have died at the site and many more would have been badly hurt.

Dream to Cure

*D*reams are being used not only to communicate or warn but to cure as well. Baba has been using them very liberally to rid His devotees of their physical ailments.

FEVER

D. M Mulgy was an atheist. In 1916 he fell seriously ill. One night an old man appeared in his dream and told him that his fever would disappear if he promised to visit Shirdi. Mulgy promised to do so and the old man disappeared. The dream frightened him so much that he woke up. On hearing about his dream, his sister-in-law showed him a picture of Baba. Mulgy was convinced that Sai Baba Himself had appeared in his dream. Soon his fever subsided and he was all right. Later, when he visited Shirdi he was struck by Baba's exact likeness to the old man of his dream.

CHICKEN POX

Once, all Mr. and Mrs. M. W. Pradhan's children had chicken pox. All except the youngest one recovered. But the condition of the youngest one was critical. He was on the verge of collapsing. One night Mrs. Pradhan dreamt that Baba was saying, "The child is all right. He will ask for something to eat at 6 a.m. Give him that without any fear." Mrs. Pradhan got up with a shock. To her surprise she found the child fast asleep but his condition seemed to be better. At the predicted time, the child asked for his meals. Within a few days he recovered fully.

CHOLERA

Mr. Shinde's neighbour was down with cholera. He gave him 'udhi' and the man was cured. As a result more people started coming to him for treatment. 'Udhi' got finished. By the time he went to a neighboring village where he was asked to treat a patient, he did not have any 'udhi'. Just to evade treating people, he demanded two hundred rupees (In those days silver coins were used.) to cure the patient. The boy's father agreed to pay even that. At this stage Baba came to his rescue. He appeared in his dream and recommended a medicine with which the boy was cured.

STOMACH ULCER

There are many instances of Baba curing stomach ulcers. Two of them are recounted here.

Mr. Jain was suffering from a stomach ulcer. He was at one place and his wife Sarojabai, at another. She was worried about her husband's health. One night she had a terrible dream. She saw her husband's body being carried to the cremation ground and she was telling her husband that she preferred death to widowhood. In the dream a strange Faqir with a radiant face said to her, "Why do you weep? Your husband will come to life again." At this, her husband sat up and the dream ended. Later, she came to know that on the same day her husband's condition had grown hopeless and that he soon recovered quite mysteriously. She later saw the picture of Sai Baba and recognized Him, as the Faqir who had come in her dream and she started worshipping Him, ignoring the criticism of her co-religionists. After some time she visited Shirdi and recognized the place where the visionary Faqir stood. It was the Dwarkamai.

In 1965, Mr. Chitnis suffered from a severe pain in the stomach and could not take even a spoonful of water. The doctors decided to try surgery on the next day. Chitnis prayed that he may be spared the ordeal of an operation. That night in his dream he saw that four persons were pulling him off the bed. Baba felled some of them and saved Chitnis. By morning Mr. Chitnis was all right to the surprise of the doctors.

FRUSTRATION

In 1942, Mrs. Mani Shankar of Mumbai was passing through a period of frustration. A neighbour brought Narsimha Swami to her place to help her to get peace. Swamiji gave her a packet of books to read and a photo of Sai Baba to worship. But Mrs. Mani Shankar was least interested in saints. One day her husband happened to read one of the books. He recommended to his wife to read those books as they might help her. Just to please her husband, she took out the photo of Baba and placed it on the table. That night, Baba appeared in her dream and blessed her with His hands. Baba's touch dispelled her frustration. Her mind was at peace and the apathy for Baba was gone.

DUMBNESS

R S Mani Eyer's daughter was dumb from birth. Mani Eyer started worshipping Baba. Once Baba appeared in his dream and instructed him to make his little daughter worship His Samadhi at Shirdi. He did accordingly and immediately she uttered the name of Sai Baba. In a short while she started speaking quite normally.

TONSILS

A priest's daughter was suffering from enlarged tonsils since her childhood and his friends told him that he must get them surgically removed at the earliest possible time. Owing to ill health even though the girl had attained marriageable age, she remained stunted in growth. His financial condition did not permit him to get her proper medical treatment. He left every thing in the hands of Sai Baba. On 12-10-1974 Baba appeared in that girl's dream and cured her. In her own words, "I was admitted in a hospital. Sai Baba appeared as the doctor and two other deities acted as a nurse and an assistant. They made me sit in a chair and He told me to open my mouth. So I did. Baba performed an operation on the spot where there was pain. When I woke up I found that

I was free from all pain and my ailment had been eradicated. It is sixteen months since I had this dream and the trouble has never reoccurred," This dream was narrated on 13-3-1976.

MIGRAINE
In March 1975, Mr. B. Ramkrishan had partial headache very frequently, but one night he had a very severe headache. That night in his dream he saw Baba emerging from the small photograph in his pocket. He sat on his right side, His hand on his head and glanced lovingly at him and then disappeared. The headache had vanished by the time he woke up.

SCIATICA and RHEUMATISM
In 1932 Mr. Purandhar was down with sciatica and rheumatism. He saw 'yamdoots' near him. But at the same time he saw Baba who came and sat on his bed, placed His hand on his head and prevented the 'yamdoots' from touching him. After the dream he got well.

CONSUMPTION
Vinayak Appaji Vaidya's wife was suffering from consumption. It was a hopeless case. Baba appeared to her in her dream and said to her that she would be all right if she visited Shirdi. After that she was taken to Shirdi. In fifteen days her fever came down. Her weight began to increase. She recovered to the extent that she was able to give birth to four children.

ACHES
Sushilamma was an uneducated, sixty-year-old woman. She had been ailing for quite some time and the complaints were many. The most prominent of these were pain in the eyes, bodyache and often, she spat blood. All the doctors of that area who examined her expressed their inability to cure her and advised her to consult specialists else where. Once she had a severe cold and fever which rendered these complaints unbearable. She was helpless. One night, before going to bed she silently prayed to Baba to cure her. Early next morning Baba appeared in her dream. He came near

her bed and squeezed the juice of some leaves into one of her ears. She helped the juice to move deeper into her ears by shaking her earlobes. The juice flowed into her mouth and it tasted very pleasant. She wished the taste to last longer, but she woke up. There was no sign of any juice poured into her ears. But the most wonderful thing is all her complaints, including the spitting of blood, had completely vanished by the next morning. She, who was unable to take proper care of herself earlier, was able to assist her grand children.

Later, on another occasion, she was all alone and started having body ache and the very next day she had to water the fields. She prayed to Baba for help. Baba appeared in her dream with castor oil in His hands. Soon she woke up and found that she was healthy and could work single-handedly to water the fields.

There is an instance of a poor ailing housewife being administered a tablet in a dream by Baba and the woman recovered her health by the next day.

Mrs. Purandhar was ill before her delivery. Baba appeared in her dream and she got well without any medication.

KIDNEY TROUBLE

On 26-6-1980 Mrs. Sneh Kiran's brother had a severe attack of kidney trouble. She wanted to give him 'udhi' but he would not accept it. All the members of the family started praying to Baba for him. At night the patient had two dreams. In one of the dreams he saw a line of 'udhi' around his bed and a lighted 'diya' in one of the corners of the room. In the second dream he saw Baba sitting on a stone and at His feet was sitting a horrible looking man who was saying, " I won't leave him." But he had to leave as Baba was there to protect the patient.

TUBERCULOSIS

Shivshankar Dixit, a devotee of Lord Dattatrey, despaired when he knew that he was suffering from tuberculosis. One day he had a dream. He saw the picture of a Muslim saint and bowed to it.

At the same moment, a Muslim Faqir came and applied 'udhi' on his forehead and assured him that he would soon get well. When his condition improved without any treatment Dixit realized it was a visitation. One of his friends suggested that the Faqir might be Sai Baba, Himself. Four days after that a group of children who played there, left a small picture of Baba's samadhi in his house. Dixit found that the Faqir of his dream precisely resembled the photograph of Sai Baba on the samadhi found in the picture. Later he visited Shirdi and saw that there was the marble statue on Baba's samadhi and not a photograph of Sai Baba. On enquiry, he was told that till 6th Oct. 1954 a photograph of Sai Baba was indeed kept on Baba's samadhi and that the statue was installed on 7-10-1954. The picture of the Muslim Faqir which he saw in his dream was indeed Baba's photograph which was earlier kept on the samadhi.

One Bheemaji Patil of Narayangaon developed tuberculosis and was often seen spitting blood. Doctors failed to cure him and finally he was directed by Nana Sahib to see Sai Baba of Shirdi. When Bheemaji arrived, Baba said that the disease was caused by the evil deeds of a past life and He was unwilling to interfere with it. But the patient wept bitterly and implored Baba for His blessings. Baba was moved and said, "Don't be afraid. Your sufferings have come to an end. Whoever steps into this Masjid, will be relieved of his sufferings, however bad they might be. The Faqir here is very kind." Soon the spitting of blood stopped and his condition took a turn for the better. Baba kept the patient in the house of one Bheemabai. The house seemed quite unhygienic. Shortly after that the patient had two dreams. In the first dream, he saw himself as a boy, being flogged by the the teacher at school for not reciting his poetry lesson. In the second dream, he saw a heavy roller moving up and down on his chest causing him intense pain. By the time he woke up his disease was completely cured. With Baba's blessing he soon left Shirdi. In gratitude for Baba's grace, Bheemaji started a new form of worship called Sai Satnarain pooja modelled on Shree Satnarain pooja.

SERIOUS ILLNESS

In September 1978 Mr. B. Adrishta Rao, a Christian, was in a troubled state of mind. One of his colleagues gave him a picture of Sai Baba and assured him that he would be relieved of his problems by merely keeping it with him. With the passage of time this Christian couple started worshipping Sai Baba.

In January 1979 his wife became seriously ill and was admitted into a government hospital. The husband had to look after their four children, the youngest among them being just five months old. The husband prayed to Baba to save them from the impending calamity. The next day, the lady opened her eyes and recounted her experience, "Baba appeared in my dream. One of my kinsman, who had recently died of cancer was trying to drag me out through the window, pulling my hand. Baba at once rushed there, dragged away the dark form of my kinsman and threw him into the blazing flames. I appealed to Baba not to be so cruel to him. Baba said, 'You don't know anything. He is solely responsible for all the hardships of your family and he should be punished. You need not fear. You will be all right in a few days.' " Indeed, within a few days she was all right.

28

Use of Voice

Baba has always been in touch with his devotees. He made use of different techniques to convey what he wanted to. At times he appeared personally before them. Sometimes he made use of a dream. He also made use of his 'voice' to contact his devotees.

Once in 1912, Mr G.K. Rege's four-year-old daughter was suffering from fever. So much so, she became a skeleton. All medical treatment failed to cure her. Her mother, a Sai devotee, prayed to Baba to help her daughter. During her prayers she heard a voice saying, "I will take away all the troubles on the third day." They were shocked when, on the third day, the girl died. The father was informed and he came home running. As is customary among the Hindus, he tried to pour 'gangajal' into her mouth. To their surprise, it did not come out. Then he gave more 'gangajal' and abhishek tirath. The girl reacted to that. She showed signs of life. Then onwards she started improving, and within a week, she was completely all right.

Mrs and Mr Rege were devotees of Sai Baba since 1910. In 1924 they went from place to place in search of a son-in-law. As they alighted at the station, Rege heard a voice clearly, "Go to Jeerapur." They spent a day or so at that place with their relatives and came back to Indore. In the meanwhile their son got transfer orders for Jeerapur but he got the posting cancelled as his wife was in an advanced stage of pregnancy and they could not move to an unknown place. Then Mr Rege got transferred to Kathgodam.

But when the transfer orders went to the officer for signatures he changed them to Jeerapur. It was here that Mr Rege was able to find his son-in-law.

Sh. Krishan Rao Narain Palekar, Honorary Magistrate of Harda, was a staunch believer in Sai Baba. For years, he had been celebrating Dattatrey Jayanti, which usually falls in December. If due to unavoidable circumstances he could not feed Brahmins, one year he would feed double the number the next year. In 1925, a Saturday was fixed for celebrations. On Tuesday as he meditated, he saw Baba urging him to invite Mr Dixit from Mumbai. He hesitated, thinking it would not be proper to bother a person to come for a meal from such a far-off place. Again, he heard a voice repeating the same instructions: "If you desire that on the day you are feeding the Brahmins, I should come and partake of the food, call Mr Dixit from Mumbai." On Wednesday, he wrote to Mr Dixit and he came along with Shama to partake the feast.

Gopal Bhaskar Dattatrey's experiences confirmed his faith in Baba. He says a lady in the house who was suffering from internal pains for a long time and had vainly tried some medicines, was listening to him as he read the *Sai Satcharita* aloud. There was the episode of Sai Baba intervening to save a frog that was caught by a snake. She heard it half-dozing. She prayed in that half-dozing state to Sai Baba, "O Sai Baba, you have pity for and help humble suffering creatures like a frog. Have you no mercy for me—a human being?" She heard a voice that seemed to come from a peg on the wall, "Will you give me five rupees as dakshina for the Dussehra celebrations?" She promised she would when she got cured. At once she woke up from her sleep, narrated her experience and wanted five rupees to be sent as her contribution for Sai Baba's Dussehra celebration. It was done immediately and by the evening her agony abated. This happened in 1931–32.

In June 1940 Sh. Jai Ram Naidu's five-year-old son was down with some ailment. That very day he brought Baba's photograph, and the husband and the wife prayed to Him for their son's recovery. At night, the wife was woken up by someone telling her,

Use of Voice

"This is no time to sleep. Look after your son." She got up and found that her son's condition had deteriorated. Timely medical aid was given and the boy began to recover.

Mr F.M. Bhatnagar, a Parsi, bought a calendar with Sai Baba's portrait and kept it in his bedroom. One day at 6 a.m. he was impelled to bow down to Baba and was surprised at his own act. He did not reveal this to his wife. The next morning, the calendar had been garlanded. When asked, his wife told him that while cleaning the photo she heard a voice, "Child, garland me regularly. It will do you good," and she obeyed it. One day this mysterious voice asked her what she wanted. She sought the welfare of her husband and the birth of a son. Within a week, of his own sweet will the senior officer recommended a raise in Mr Bhatnagar's salary. In June 1957 they were blessed with a son.

Sh. Santosh Vyas of Hoshangabad was going to Shirdi. It was the first day of October 1980. The train started moving. All of a sudden Mr Vyas heard an urgent voice asking him to get down and occupy another compartment. In obedience to the command, he got down and entered a rear compartment, fourteenth from the engine. Very soon, his train collided with a goods train, resulting in a large number of casualties in the third compartment, which Mr Vyas had vacated.

29

Baba's Grace

Baba's generosity and bounty knew no bounds. There is neither a beginning nor an end to his grace. His treasure is inexhaustible and He is always showering it on His devotees.

G. Laxminarain was a frequent visitor to Shirdi during Baba's time. Once, Baba asked him to build a temple of Laxmi Narain, costing six hundred thousand rupees. G. Laxminarain was aghast as he was an ordinary merchant. But within two years, his business flourished to such an extent that he got a temple built at Secunderabad. Of course, by that time Baba had taken mahasamadhi.

In 1930, Sh. Rai Bahadur Dhumal, another devotee of Sai Baba, was having his meals when head of the department entered his office. Sh. Dhumal apologized for not being able to get up to give proper welcome to the dignitary. The chief did not mind and went into the room where there was Sai Baba's photograph. For a while he gazed at the photo and then came out. Unasked, he announced an increment of fifty rupees for Sh. Dhumal.

In 1942–43 Dr A.R. Govind Rao treated Promila—a case of burns. It took him six months to cure her. Then he was transferred. At his farewell, the girl's father gave him 'udhi' and a photograph of Baba. With the passage of time, the doctor forgot about this incident. In 1952–53 when he was in Mysore, there was a sudden downpour and he and his brother-in-law took shelter in the nearest building which happened to be a Sai temple. At that time arati and pooja were going on. The doctor was reminded of the arati and pooja at Promila's house. The pujari of the temple gave him a photograph of Baba to be kept in his own house. He could not think of owning a house as he had only five thousand rupees in his bank account. Baba wanted him to have his own house, and a cooperative society came up. It demanded only five thousand rupees as an initial deposit and the rest in easy instalments over a period of twenty years. By 1954 the doctor had the possession of his own house, where he installed the photograph given by the pujari of the Mysore temple.

Two devotees of Baba purchased a copy each of Baba's photograph. On the way they realized that they should have purchased another copy for their friend. On reaching home when they opened their packet of photos, to their surprise there were three copies instead of the two! They definitely ascribed it to Baba's grace.

A thief broke into the house of a Railway Telegraph Master, Rattan Lal of Vani, and was rifling through the valuables. A child cried out suddenly and the thief's leg hit a bucket. Rattan Lal woke up and ran after the thief. By Baba's grace he lost nothing.

30

Baba and the Low-Caste

*B*aba never differentiated between the rich and the poor or the high and the low. During his lifetime Baba visited only two houses, one of which was of Bhikhu, the drunkard when he was ill. His motherless daughter approached Baba for help. The girl was not allowed to step into the Dwarkamai as she was an untouchable. But Baba Himself went to his house and looked after him.

Once, Septnaker was pressing Baba's legs. A low-caste shepherdess pushed him aside and started pressing Baba's legs. Baba accepted her services with pleasure. He never objected to the shepherdess' act, though the high-caste Septnaker must have felt humiliated.

Baba never wanted even beggars to insulted. Once Mr Sathe committed this mistake. He brushed aside a foul-smelling beggar woman and was penalized for that. He missed his train and had to spend boring twenty-four hours at the station. A fellow passenger told Mr Sathe how he had met a foul-smelling beggar woman and given her alms. The moment he gave her alms he felt elated. This was so because the moment the beggar woman turned her back, the place was full of the sweet smell of flowers. This was enough to make Mr Sathe realize that he was being punished for insulting a low-caste beggar woman.

Once Dass Ganu went to Baba and requested that he might send Bala Patel to be his guest. Bala Patel was of low caste. He knew Baba would not care to go to his house and have His dinner there. So Baba, in granting his request, said, "Don't cry 'dhat-dhat' at him" (i.e. "Do not humiliate him by giving a place far away from your own seat while eating). Dass Ganu made Bala Patel sit near him and not outside the house.

Baba and Onion

Most Hindus look down upon onions. They believe it to be part of 'tamsik bhojan' and they reject it on the grounds of its odour. But Dass Ganu says that Baba had a very high opinion of onions. If one can digest it, it does no harm but good. Baba himself used to eat raw onions as part of his meal. He made Dass Ganu eat onion on most days other than 'Ekadashi'.

Once a 'yogabhyasi' Brahmin came to Shirdi with Nana Sahib Chandorkar. He wanted to get some more hints about yogabhyas from Baba but was stunned to see Baba eating chappati with raw onion. He doubted how much Baba, who ate raw onion, could teach him. Promptly came Baba's response to his unspoken thoughts, "Nana, only those who can digest onions should eat them." This was enough to make him believe in Baba's, divinity even though He ate raw onion.

Once an old woman came to see Baba. Baba wanted to know what she had brought for him. She had brought only one chappati and two onions. Half of it she had eaten on the way and the rest she gave to Baba, who relished it very much. He found it very delicious.

Once Shanta Ram Balwant Nachane's mother-in-law was cutting onions for cooking. Mr Kalekar, a Brahmin, looked down upon her for eating onions. The lady did not react to the insult. In the afternoon when Kalekar went to the Dwarkamai, he took his granddaughter with him as she had a severe earache and he wanted Baba to cure it. Baba recommended onion juice as medicine. Mr

Kalekar wondered where to get it from. Baba pointed to the lady whom Kalekar had insulted for eating onions. On the one hand, Baba wanted to humble his pride and on the other hand he wanted to emphasize that there is nothing 'tamsik' about onions. They have great medicinal values.

32

When Permission to Depart was not Granted

*O*ne speciality of the Shirdi pilgrimage was that none could leave Shirdi without Baba's permission and if he did, he invited trouble. If any one was asked to leave Shirdi, he could no longer stay there. Baba gave certain suggestions or hints, when devotees went to bid goodbye and take leave. If they were not followed or were departed from, accidents were sure to befall them. If people didn't heed Baba's words they had to suffer.

One morning, Nana Sahib Chandorkar went to Baba to seek permission to go to Kopergaon to meet the District Collector who was expected there on some official business. Baba refused permission saying, "Go tomorrow." It was an important engagement which Nana could ill afford not to keep but relying on Baba's words, he did not go to Kopergaon. The next day when Nana went to Baba, He told him, "Now you can go and meet your Collector at Kopergaon." Nana went to Kopergaon and enquired from his staff what had happened the previous day and was told that the Collector had sent a telegram, saying he would come to Kopergaon the following day. So Chandorkar was saved from the twenty-four hours' torturous wait and he got time to be with Baba.

In 1913, Kaka Dixit was at Shirdi. He received a letter that his son was sick and that he should come back to Mumbai to look after his ailing son. When he went to Baba to seek permission, Baba asked him to send for his son. So his ailing son was brought to Shirdi where medical facilities were nil. Any way the boy recovered without any medicine. Then this boy was to appear for an examination to be held on 2-11-1913 but Baba would not let him go. Ultimately the examination was postponed to 6-11-1913. Still Baba did not let him go back home. Everyone was worried but nobody could disobey Baba. Once again, the examination was postponed to 13-11-1913. Then Baba allowed him to go back. He went back appeared in the examination and got through. Nobody suffered because he was refused permission to leave Shirdi.

Raghubir Purandhar, a railway employee, came to Shirdi in 1912. Baba detained him beyond his official leave. When Shyama or any one else pleaded his case that his boss would be annoyed Baba used to say, "I am his boss". After overstaying his leave, when he reached his office the foreman asked Purandhar where he had been and reported his unauthorized absence to his boss. Purandhar immediately handed in his resignation. When his boss asked him where he had been during that period, Purandhar simply told the truth that he was with Baba. His boss, Mr. Curtis, knew that nobody could leave Shirdi without Baba's permission. So, he tore up his resignation letter. The foreman was helpless to do him any harm. The irony of the situation, is that within six months Purandhar was promoted and the foreman became his subordinate.

In 1909, Mr. Hari Vinayak Sathe had to attend an important meeting at Manmad. He sent Mr. Kalekar, his father-in-law, to seek permission on his behalf. But Baba would not grant permission. Mr. Kalekar went back and told him about the refusal. He sent his father-in-law again to tell Baba that the meeting was so important that he could be thrown out of the Government job if he missed it. But Baba would not listen to any argument. Instead, He asked Mr. Kalekar to lock Sathe up in a room lest he should leave without His permission. Sathe was locked-up for three days. He went to Manmad with a palpitating heart but was surprised to know that the original programme had been postponed for three days. Sathe did not lose anything by his detention at Shirdi for three days.

Vithal Vaidya, a railway employee, was anxious to return home and join duty in the office the next day. But Baba detained him for hours together when he went to seek permission. After a delay of four hours Baba let him go but he felt it was useless going to the station as the train he had intended to board must have left hours back. But others told him that since Baba had given him permission, he must leave. So, he had to go to the Kopergaon station. When he reached the station he was surprised to see the train he had intended to catch, coming into the platform. The train was late by five hours. He was happy to reach his destination in time without wasting time in a torturous wait for the train.

Bapu Sahib Jog had lent two–three thousand rupees to a man in Ahmadnagar. He wanted to go there to collect his money but Baba would not let him go. Jog was so enraged by this that he threatened to stop Baba's 'arati' and 'pooja'. But Baba would not budge an inch. Jog was expected to sit and wait for the man to come to Shirdi and return the money to him. Poor Jog was helpless. He had to obey Baba. There came a day when the debtor himself came and returned the principal sum.

Once Jog wanted to perform the 'shradh' ceremony of his deceased father. He wanted to go to Kopergaon to find a suitable Brahmin to perform the ceremony at Shirdi. But Baba refused permission. He requested Baba again to let him go as only two days were left for the ceremony. Baba told him to sit quietly as Brahmins would be coming to perform the ceremony. Jog was helpless as nobody could leave Shirdi without Baba's permission. On the day when the ceremonies were to be performed two Brahmins came for Baba's 'darshan'. Before they left they asked Baba if they could get Brahmin food in Shirdi. Baba directed them to Jog's house. Jog was very pleased for they were Brahmins of his own caste and quite well-versed in rituals and with their help Jog succeeded in doing 'shradh' for the soul of his father.

The classic case of detention was that of Sh. G. S. Kharparde. His detention exceeded a hundred days!. It was his second visit to Shirdi. In spite of the persistent desire of Khaparde and his wife to go back to Amrawati, Sai Baba detained them in Shirdi and would not let them go. Since Khaparde had implicit faith in Sai Baba he dutifully obeyed His order believing and knowing that Baba's decision was in his interest. Since Khaparde had been agitating for the release of Lokmanya Tilak, he was on the hit list of the government and his arrest was imminent. Baba must have foreseen this for nothing in this world was unknown to Him or escaped His attention. If you go through Khaparde's diary it says on 18-1-1912, "During the torrent of hard words that Sai Maharaj poured out today He said that He had saved my son, Balwant and then often repeated the phrase, "Faqir (God) wishes to kill Dada Sahib (meaning me) but I would not permit it." It becomes more than clear that the detention was to protect his favourite devotee's life. Once, Baba told Mrs. Kharparde that the governor had come with a lance. Baba had a 'trishul' and with that he had driven him out. Khaparde's son in his father's biography interprets the lance of the governor as the arrest warrants and the 'trishul' as Baba's grace.

Balkrishan Waman Vaidya says that when they sought permission to leave Shirdi, Baba said, "You had better leave tomorrow." But they could not prolong their trip. So they left for the station. But by the time they reached Manmad the train had left. They felt sad as they had to spend the night at the station. Imagine their grateful surprise when they learnt that the previous train to Bombay, which they had intended to board, had met with an accident. Baba's watchful eyes had saved His children from harm in that accident.

Bapusahib Dhumal had to attend an important case at Naphed. On the way he halted at Shirdi to have Baba's 'darshan' and 'udhi'. When he had had both, he wanted to proceed to Naphed as he had intended only a fleeting stopover at Shirdi but Baba detained him for one full week! But Dhumal was not a loser in any way as the Magistrate who was to decide the case had developed pain in the stomach. The case had to be postponed for a week.

In October 1918, Dhumal received a letter from Pune from his brother that his wife (Dhumal's sister-in-law) was seriously ill and that he should immediately come to his house. Without wasting time Dhumal left Nasik for Pune with sufficient funds in his pocket. On the way he halted at Shirdi to seek Baba's blessings and 'udhi'. Baba depleted him of all his money by asking him for 'dakshina' very frequently. He detained him for full three days. Dhumal was helpless. Whenever he went to Baba to seek permission to leave Shirdi, Baba in His typical style would say, "We'll see tomorrow." On the third day, he got the intimation that his sister-in-law had left for her heavenly abode. Then Baba allowed him to go. Dhumal was not a loser. He got a few days to be with Baba as shortly after that Baba too left this world.

Nobody suffered if he obeyed Baba.

Those who obeyed Baba's instructions or followed hints were safe and sound. Those who ignored His words met with accidents in one way or the other.

Tatya Kote Patil was once going in a tonga to Kopergaon. He came in haste to the Mosque, saluted Baba and said that he was going to the Kopergaon market. Baba said, "Don't make haste. Stop a little and forget the market. Don't go out of the village." On seeing his anxiety to go, Baba asked him to take Shyama with him. Not minding this instruction, Tatya Kote immediately drove off his tonga. Of the two horses, one which cost him Rs. 300 was very active and restless. After some time, it began to run rashly, got a sprain in its waist and fell down. Tatya was not much hurt but was reminded of Baba's directions. On another occasion also his tonga met with an accident when he disregarded Baba's directions.

One Rambhau Londhe of Astegaon village invited Mhalsapati to his house for a special lunch and to read the Mhalsapati Puran. But when he went to Baba to take leave, Baba said to him, "Don't go. There will be a fight there." But Mhalsapati loathe to miss a rare chance in life, went to that place, not heeding Baba's words. Sitting on a decorated pedestal there, he began to read his Puran with an uncommon zeal. Meanwhile, when the Puran reading was going on some boys sat for meals and they began exchanging heated words. From words they came to blows, sticks and heavy cudgels. The elders also joined them. There was a regular fight. People started leaving. Mhalsapati, too, had to take to his heels. He was in tears when he went to Baba and narrated his experience of the day. "Baba, your words proved true to the letter and I should have heeded your words of wisdom," said he.

Once Thomas, a European officer, went to Shirdi. He had an introduction letter from Nana Sahib Chandorkar. He wanted to kneel before Baba and kiss His hand in a true European, manner. It was Thursday. The Dwarkamai was over crowded. Every time he wanted to enter the Mosque he was asked to wait. Displeased with the treatment, he bade Him goodbye. But Baba told him to leave the next day and not to hurry. People present in the Mosque requested him to obey Baba but the man whose vanity had been rudely shocked, paid no heed and left Shirdi for Mumbai via Kopergaon. The horses of his tonga at first ran well and fast but after some time the animals, beacause they sighted a bicycle, a rare sight in those days, got very frightened and they suddenly started running very fast, overturning the vehicle. The occupant fell down on the road and was actually dragged some distance. He was rescued by the passersby. But he had to be hospitalised till his wounds healed.

Ganpati Teli, an honorary magistrate of Thane, went to Shirdi accompanied by a nurse. When they begged leave from Baba to leave Shirdi, Baba said, "You have come. Why not stay here some more time?" But the nurse pleaded some previous, urgent engagement. So both the magistrate and the nurse left Shirdi the same day. When the nurse reached home she found that thieves had broken into her house and carried away lots of valuables.

In 1912, Tukaram Bakru wanted to go to Karanjigaon, a village 20 miles away from Shirdi to eke out his living and when he was about to start Baba met him on the way and putting His arm around his shoulders and advised him not to go to that village. Tukaram, however, did not pay heed to the advice and went away only to be attacked by fever the next day and he had to lie in bed for over a month and a half. Working was out of question and he had to depend upon the kindness of some relatives who looked after him.

Nurudeen came to Baba, took His 'darshan' and wanted to leave. Baba said to him, "Go tomorrow." This meant he was denied permission. He showed his inability to prolong his visit because of his job. Baba gave him 'udhi' and at the same time said, "Dig a pit and eat the 'udhi'" The man took 'udhi' and rode away. At Kopergaon he saw a corpse being carried away. After that he had a sumptuous meal. He started having a vision of a corpse very frequently. On days when he had such a vision he got food and dined to his satisfaction. On days on which he did not get the vision of the corpse, try as he might, he failed to have his food for some reason or the other. This mortified him so much that he gave up his job because of which he had to leave Shirdi without Baba's clear cut permission. He realized that the curse was because of his failure to stay back with Baba. So, he returned to Baba and stayed at Shirdi for full six months. Then the curse left him. He led a normal life when he left Shirdi with Baba's permission.

In those days of plague Abdul Rahim Rangari went to Shirdi because his wife had some throat problem and swelling on the cheeks—sure symptoms of plague. She could neither eat nor drink anything. A lawyer neighbour advised him to take his wife to Shirdi Sai Baba. As soon as they started the journey the patient started feeling better. By the time they reached Shirdi the trouble had practically gone, Rangari's object had been achieved. So he did not want to stay in that unknown place unnecessarily with his wife and child. Without seeking Baba's permission he went out and hired a tonga for the station. On the way at 10 p.m. the tonga broke down. They could neither go ahead nor come back. There was the danger of being molested and robbed. At midnight, they heard the rumble of a carriage and the coachman crying, "Thanewala! Thanewala!" Rangari told the coachman that he was from Thane. On enquiry he came to know that Baba had sent the

When Permission to Depart was not Granted 199

coach to fetch them back to Shirdi. It was already 2 a.m. when they reached the Dwarkamai. They spent the rest of the night there. In the morning Rangari expressed regret for not seeking permission before departing. After that Baba went out on His begging spree. He brought bread which He shared with the Rangari family. Now Mrs. Rangari could chew the bread. There was no problem when they left Shirdi after seeking Baba's permission.

Amir Shakhar, a butcher by caste, was suffering from sciatica. When all remedies failed to give him any relief he came to Shirdi Sai Baba for help. Baba advised him to put up in the Chavadi which was in a dilapidated condition. He obeyed Baba and stayed there for nine months. He got cured due to Baba's company as Baba used to sleep there on alterate nights. When he was completely cured he felt there was no need for him to stay in that dingy place any more. One night he left the place without Baba'a permission and felt like a man recently released from prison. He reached an inn and wanted to rest there. Here he found a faqir on his death bed and crying for water. He took pity on the unfortunate faqir's plight and gave him some water to drink. The faqir immediately breathed his last. Now he was all alone in the company of a corpse. Though he was innocent he could easily be taken for a murderer and could be behind bars till the trial was over and his innocence was proved. The thought was too much for him to digest. He took to his heels and reached the Chavadi like a fugitive from the police. He promised to himself never to leave the safety provided by Baba.

On the way to Ahmadnagar Nana Sahib Chandorkar along with Ramdasi and one other friend halted at Shirdi. After taking Baba's 'darshan' Ramdasi Bua wanted to leave Shirdi immediately. He did not want to miss his 'kirtan' the next day at Ahmadnagar during the festival of Hanuman Jayanti and lose his money. So, when they went to Baba to get His permission to leave Shirdi, Baba asked them to take their meals and then go to Kopergaon station. Nana agreed to stay behind and take his meal and his friend Kangnaokar also followed suit. But the 'karaka' knowing fully the timings of the train thought if he stayed he would miss his train. He did not heed Baba's words and hurried to Kopergaon station well in time. But the train was late by three hours and he had to starve on the platform. Meanwhile, Nana Chandorkar and Kangnaokar had their meals and came to the station after getting Baba's leave. Chandorkar and his friend were saved from the tortuous wait for the train. Ramdasi suffered because he did not pay heed to Baba's words.

In fact, no body could step into Shirdi or leave Shirdi without Baba's permission. He could stay in Shirdi only as long as Baba desired. If He wanted a person to go, he had to leave. If he listened to what Baba said he was benefited. But if he ignored His words, he had to suffer.

Once, Das Ganu and Bere were to leave Shirdi for Kopergaon to catch a train for which there was plenty of time. When they went to take leave, Baba in giving leave said, "Start at once. Don't stop. Go straight to Kopergaon." They acted on His advice. Other coachmen told them to wait and go with them on that dangerous road to have the benefit of their company. They, however, followed Baba's instructions and drove straight on and arrived safely at the Kopergaon station. The coachmen who came latter were in time to catch the train but had been waylaid by robbers. Baba's advice saved Das Ganu and Bere from that mishap.

Kaka Mahajani of Mumbai went to Shirdi to spend a full week there and to participate in the Gokul Ashtami celebrations. But the moment he saw Baba, He said, "When are you returning home?" Kaka Mahajani was surprised by this unwanted and unexpected question. Still, he said that he would go whenever he was asked or ordered to go. Then Baba said, "Go tomorrow." So, the next day he left for Mumbai as ordered by Baba. When he came to his office in Mumbai, his boss was waiting for him as the manager had suddenly fallen ill and his presence was badly needed in Mumbai. So much so that a letter had been sent to him at his Shirdi address requesting him to come back immediately. That letter was redirected and reached him only after he had reached home.

When Permission to Depart was not Granted

Balkrishan Vaidya, a railway employee, went to Baba with his entire family and stayed there for 4 to 5 days. When he went to Baba to seek permission to leave Shirdi, Baba said, "You had better go now" and gave him 'udhi' and blessings. He immediately took a tonga and reached the station. But he was sad to know that the train he wanted to board had just steamed off. He had to spend the night on the platform. The next day he was shocked to learn that the train he had missed, had met with an accident. He thanked Baba for saving him.

Yashwantrao, grandson of Raghunath Mukund, an engineer, went to Shirdi with Raghunath Purandhar, a devotee of Baba, on the occasion of the Guru Purnima in the month of June. The cholera epidemic was raging fiercely in Shirdi. Yashwantrao did not wish to leave Shirdi before Raghunath Purandhar did. So, when Baba told him to go away and gave him 'udhi' he did not leave Shirdi even when Purandhar advised him to go. The result was Yashwantrao had an attack of cholera that very night and he succumbed to it early next morning.

Hindu–Muslim Unity

Sh. S.P. Ruhela in his book *Sri Shirdi Sai Baba*, says, "After the death of Faqir, the Faqiri was at her tether's end. The child, christened Babu was always up to strange and abnormal acts, offensive to her religion. He would go to the Hindu temples and recite the Quran or install a stone "Shivling" in a mosque and worship it. He would sing songs in praise of Allah in Hindu shrines and say Ram is God and Shiv is Allah and so on and so forth. Puzzled at such behaviour and with scores of daily complaints from the Hindus and the Muslims against Babu, she eventually decided to take Babu to Selam and entrust him to the charge of a pious and spiritually elevated guru Venkusa who was running an ashram for orphaned, abandoned and poor boys of all communities."

Rangaswami Parthsarthy in his book *God Who Walked on Earth*, says, "Baba was a living emblem of Hindu–Muslim unity. His life and teachings were the strangest expression of the underlying unity of all communities and creeds in India. There were elements of both Hinduism and Islam, so closely intermingled in Him that a conclusion was not easy. Two years before his mahasamadhi, Baba threw off his clothes and stood naked, asking the curious people to see whether he was a Hindu or a Muslim. Some devotees noticed that Baba had his ear lobes pierced, an indication that he was a Hindu."

Shri E. Bhardwaj in his book *Sai Baba the Master*, says, "The life of Sai Baba is unique. He does not merely teach about the omnipresent spirit. Indeed His verbal teaching is minimum as mere verbal teaching cannot strike deep in the heart of the common man. He, therefore, taught through direct experiences. To the Hindus He was an orthodox Brahmin with the sacred fire enjoining the worship of many gods and the devout study of various Hindu scriptures. He even named the mosque as Dwarkamai and planted tulsi plant in its frontyard and He allowed Himself to be worshipped by His devotees in a Hindu fashion. To the Muslims he was a 'pir' living in a mosque observing the discipline enjoined for a faqir always uttering the Islamic "Allah Malik". To the Parsis He was the sacred fire worshipper. In Him, there was perfect harmony of all religions."

Alison Williams in his book *Experiencing Sai Baba's Shirdi*, says, "'I look on all with an equal eye,' said Baba, and He would brook no dispute or religious bigotry among His devotees. Baba expressed Himself as a Hindu to the Hindus and as a Muslim to the Muslims. However, in most cases Baba acted vice-a-versa, insisting that the Hindus should accept Him as a faqir and the Muslims as a Brahmin. The Hindus could claim Baba as their own as he responded to their needs and permitted worship according to their rituals but they could not deny the fact that his dwelling place was a mosque and the name of Allah was ever on His lips."

Baba is often described as a living emblem of Hindu–Muslim unity. The provision of a tulsi plant in a Muslim place of worship is an example of the many ways in which Baba fused Hindu and Muslim elements and desisted from being identified exclusively with one religion.

The day when Baba took samadhi, Tuesday, 15th October 1918, was a very auspicious one for the Hindus. It was Vijaydashmi. It also happened to be the Muslim month of Ramzan. In fact, Baba was embracing both the communities.

Sh. M.W. Pradhan in *Sai Baba of Shirdi*, says, "In the Dwarkamai, there were a couple of grinding stones where occasionally He used to grind corn and pulses. And in doing that he was assisted by the village women as well as high-caste Hindu and Mohammedan lady visitors who happened to be there, without the slightest feeling of caste, creed and untouchability."

Some of the most orthodox Hindu Shastris, Christians, Parsis and Mohammedan Maulvis, even butchers from Bandra, Mumbai vied with each other in paying obeisance to Him.

Baba begged food from different houses. He also got offerings from visitors. Those He mixed up and distributed Himself to some of the devotees, among whom were Mohammedans, high-caste Hindus and Parsis.

When a Mohammedan visitor came up to pay his respects, 'fatwah' was uttered. All the while Hindu devotees sitting there witnessed this 'fatwah' and partook of the lumps of sugar as well as pieces of coconut with pleasure and joy.

The Dwarkamai, owing to the sacred fire, was a temple to the most orthodox Hindus; owing to the riches, it appeared as a masjid and owing to the sound of bells, a church to the Christians. So, in this unique place all the principal creeds of the world were united and the common worship of God brought home to each and everyone in a unique and loving manner. Baba created an atmosphere of universal tolerance, goodwill and unity in a practical manner.

Perin S. Baruch in his book *Sai Baba of Shirdi*, says, "He burnt little earthenware oil lamps inside the Mosque as is done in Hindu temples. His favourite expression (Allah Malik—meaning God is the Master), however, was of Muslim origin.

The Muslims claimed Him as one of their pirs and the Hindu followers regarded Him as an incarnation of various deities in their religion.

Sai Baba Himself actively discouraged speculation among His devotees as to His identity and background because amity between the Hindus and the Muslims was a cause dear to His heart.

His Hindi was as fluent as his Urdu. Though His ears were pierced in Hindu tradition, He was a forceful advocate of the Muslim circumcision. Though He lived in the Mosque, He always had a fire burning in it. He not only had oil lamps burning night and day, He even permitted the blowing of conches and ringing of bells inside the mosque—practices that are contrary to the tenets of Islam.

In *Shri Sai the Superman*, Swami Sai Sharananand says, "He knew that among the people of the various races who visited Him something like hereditary antipathy existed, particularly between the Hindus and the Muslims, and this very often burst out in riots and murders, arson and loot. And it seems that if He had opted to adopt some of both their ways of life and religion, His object was to draw to Him the people of both these religions, to provide for them a common background for meeting and worship so that all misunderstandings would vanish and their attention would be drawn to one universal feature of devotion, common to both the religions."

The annual fair of Ram Naumi gave the Hindus and the Muslims an opportunity to meet and understand one another as a result thereof each gave up the disgust and hatred he had for the other and looked upon each other's way of worship with eyes of tolerance.

The non-Muslim devotees firmly believed that if Sai Baba had adopted Hindu–Muslim mixed ways of life and prayer it was simply for the purpose of drawing the attention of the devotee to the cardinal truth that the soul has no caste or creed.

In *Life History of Shri Sai Baba*, Sh. Ammula Sambasiva Rao says, "Venkusa was a Hindu. He did not practise discrimination on account of religion, caste or creed. All were equal to him. He used to take Baba to the samadhis of great persons of both the religions and explain their teachings and theory in detail."

Dakshina

The sacred ancient books of the Hindus laid down that worship of the gods was incomplete unless a gold coin formed part of the ritual offering. It was argued that if a coin was necessary in the worship of a god, it was also necessary when worshipping a saint. Hindu scriptures of a later date therefore stipulated that when calling on a god, king or guru one should not go empty handed. Such monetary offerings are known as 'dakshina.'

Money is said to be a symbol of attachment. Some saints avoided touching it lest it should taint their spiritual attainments which they had obtained after severe penance. In the beginning, after Sai Baba settled down in the Shirdi Mosque He never asked anything from anybody but simply stored burnt out match sticks and collected them almost as a hobby. If at times some one placed a pice or two before him, He took the same and purchased oil for the lamps or for tabacco for smoking or fuel for burning the 'dhooni' in the Mosque, but if a bigger coin was offered to Him, He refused to accept the same and immediately returned the coin to the giver, without a word. Later, when people were convinced that Baba was not just a raving faqir but a person with supernatural powers, they began to worship Him and worship without 'dakshina' would not bring fruit to the devotee. So, in the last decade of His life Baba accepted 'dakshina' so as not to displease His devotees. Not only did He accept money from His devotees but often asked for 'dakshina' and more 'dakshina' and still more dakshina until His devotee gave all his money and became a pauper. During this period He is known to have collected so much 'dakshina' from His devotees that even an income tax officer was sent to check His accounts as His income exceeded that of a governor.

It is true that Sai Baba demanded money from people but it was never money for its own sake. Nor did He ask it of every body. When He did ask for a specific amount the quantum was always symbolic. In fact 'dakshina' was a means of teaching lessons to specific devotees. If He asked for a specific sum He was not asking for money at all.If He asked any one for two rupees, He was, in fact, asking for the twin coins of faith and patience. (shradha and saburi) Baba repeatedly asked R. B. Purandhar for two rupees only. When asked why he always asked for only two rupees Baba said, "Do you think I want money? No! I want the two coins of faith and perseverance,"

If He asked some one for three rupees the amount in the case of that particular individual symbolized the surrender of lust, anger and avarice, while with another person the same sum could be symbolic of a pledge to practice charity, compassion and self control.

When Sai Baba repeatedly asked Mrs. Tarkhand, a devotee from Mumbai, for a sum of six rupees as 'dakshina' though He knew she had no money on her, she was both pained and embarrassed until her husband explained to her that it was not cash which Sai Baba was demanding of her but surrender of six enemies---lust, pride greed envy etc. Sai Baba who overheard the conversation, agreed.

Prof. Narke also had the 'dakshina' experience. He was the most highly qualified son-in-law of a millionaire, Mr. Booty. Baba was repeatedly asking him for fifteen rupees as 'dakshina'. Narke was helpless as he was out of job and Baba was fully aware of it. When they were alone Narke asked Baba why He pestered him for 'dakshina' when He knew fully well that he was broke. At this Baba told Narke as he was reading 'Yogvashishth', he should give Him fifteen rupees as 'dakshina' for that. Narke realized that getting money out of it meant deriving lessons from there and giving money to Baba meant, of course, lodging the lessons in the heart where Baba lived.

Once, Baba took away all the money that Narke had on him and still wanted seven rupees more. When Narke told Him that he didn't have it, Baba asked him to borrow it from somebody. This was a valuable lesson for him in humility. He must not consider himself too high to beg or borrow. Narke felt that Baba had pulled down his pride and egoism which otherwise would have soared so high as to avoid contact with the lower strata of society.

Once, Shamrao Jaykar, the painter, Dixit and Nimonkar were sitting in the Dwarkamai. Baba said to Jaykar, "Give Me four." Jaykar had only three rupees in his pocket and that amount was for his household expenses and Baba knew all this. Dixit looked at Jaykar questiongly wondering why he offered three rupees when Baba was asking for four. The demand for four seemed to Jaykar to indicate His desire that he should develop a sense of resignation to fate and to face utter absence of financial resources with courage and confidence.

Mr. M. B. Rege had the following experiences in 1912. He took hundred rupees with him to Shirdi. Sai Baba asked him for 'dakshina' of forty rupees. He readily gave it. A little later He asked for forty rupees more as 'dakshina' and that, too, he gave with equal readiness. Then, Baba demanded twenty rupees more. That also, he gave. But Baba was still not satisfied with that. He wanted more. When Rege said he had no money left He asked him to borrow it from Shyama. Rege approached Shyama and explained the whole situation to him. Shyama told him that Baba never cared for money. He wanted a mind, heart and soul devoted to Him. Rege then told Baba the remarks made by Shyama. Baba asked him to go to Dixit. When he approached Mr. Dixit for a loan to be given to Baba as 'dakshina', he made him understand that Baba wanted him to realize that he should not feel humiliated even if he had to beg. Mr. Rege told Baba what Mr. Dixit had told him. Baba asked him to go to Nana Sahib Chandorkar, who when acquainted with the situation gave him practical advice that is to do what he, a worldly-wise man had been doing. "Whenever I come to Shirdi I start with a certain sum and leave half of that sum at Kopergaon with a friend of mine. I had started with two hundred rupees and out of that I have left hundred rupees at Kopergaon. It is very painful to say 'No' when Baba asks for His 'dakshina'. I go on giving Him 'dakshina' out of the money in hand. When that is finished, I send for the reserve from Kopergaon. you must follow my strategy to avoid a similar fate in future,"said Chandorkar. After this guidance Rege went back to Baba and narrated what Nana had said. After that Rege was not sent out again. Now it was Chandorkar's turn to be depleted of his resources. All his money was taken away by Baba as 'dakshina' and still Baba wanted more. There was no time to send for money from Kopergaon. Thereby, Baba made him realize that no one should presume that he could supply all Baba's needs.

Kashi Ram, too, was taught the same lesson. He used to provide tobacco for Baba to smoke His chillum, besides he used to give money for the fuel of the 'dhooni'. In those days Baba did not accept any 'dakshina' as He did in the later years but still occasionally He took a pice or two a day from Kashi Ram Shimpi. Kashi Ram used to bring to Him all the money he had earned each month and request Baba to take as much money as He liked for His daily expense. He always prayed to Baba to take money from him and whenever Baba refused, he shed tears. Baba did not like this. He wanted to teach him a lesson. Baba wanted him to realize that he could not fulfill all His needs. Soon, however, Kashi Ram became a poor man and could not give what Baba asked for, so his ego and vanity were all gone. He realized that he was wrong in thinking that he could cater to all the needs of Baba. As soon as this realization dawned on Kashi Ram, his position greatly improved and once again he became a rich man.

Baba used to exhaust the finances of many people. R. B. Purandhar and others asked Baba why He behaved in that way. At this Baba replied, "I am not asking every body. I ask only from the men whom the Faqir (God) points out. But in exchange I have to give ten times the money I collect." Rasane, too, echoes the same idea. He says that Baba used to say. "He who gives Me one, to him I give two. He who gives Me two, to him I give five. He who gives Me five, I give him ten."

On the first day of his visit to Shirdi, Baba extended both His palms towards Balkrishan Upasani, Upasani Baba's brother, for 'dakshina'. The man replied that he had nothing with him to give. Then on the second day when Upasani went to Him to take His leave, Baba asked him for 'dakshina' again and Upasani again excused himself saying that he had only the necessary railway fare for his return journey home. Baba, then, pointed to the silver watch hanging on the pocket of his coat and asked for it as His 'dakshina'. Upasani at once gave it but not without a little, momentary regret and hesitation. Baba took the watch in His hands and handed it over immediately to the faqir standing by His side. Then, looking at Upasani and evidently, to allay the feeling of regret at the loss of the watch, He said to him, "You are not going to be worse off. Don't worry." Upasani replied, "Of course, Baba, it is nothing that I have given you." He left for home via Kopergaon and reached Pune. There he went to his friend's house. He talked of his recent visit to Shirdi and told his friend how Baba had taken away his watch as 'dakshina' and enquired how much it would cost to purchase a similar watch. Just then one of his friends sent his own gold watch worth about sixty rupees as a present. Balkrishan Upasani was not as Baba had said, any worse off, for parting with his watch and giving it as 'dakshina' to Baba.

Ramchander Dev alias Balabhau, another beneficiary, recounts his benefits. He says that he had funds for constructing only five rooms but Baba drew twenty-five lines on the floor and wanted twenty-rupees, that is one rupee for each line. So Dev gave twenty-five rupees as 'dakshina' and came back from Shirdi. Thereafter, he began construction work at Andheri, Mumbai and suites were slowly added to the original five, till at last their number reached twenty-five.

Dakshina

Somnath Deshpande, Nana Sahib Nimonkar's son, used to send two rupees each month from the day he got his first salary and this went on till 1920. Once during Baba's time Somnath and Nana Nimonkar went to Shirdi. Baba asked Somnath for 'dakshina' of ten rupees and it was readily given. The demand of 'Dakshina' by Baba and its payment by Somnath appeared to have no meaning then but six months later, he got an order that his salary was increased by ten rupees from the date he had paid his 'dakshina' to Baba at Shirdi.

One Purshotam Avasthi, a judicial officer, was to perform the wedding of his son. During the summer vacation on the way to the bride's house, he along with his wife and son halted at Shirdi. They had seven hundred rupees in all with them. At first, Baba demanded from him thirty rupees. Then He asked for forty rupees from his wife and then forty rupees from his son. This went on. Ultimately they were left with thirty rupees only. Baba wanted this paltry sum also. With great anguish in his heart he took the last thirty rupees from his wife and gave them to Baba. This penniless family met Jog on the way and acquainted him with the frequent demands of 'dakshina' by Baba. Jog told him that they were lucky as He always gave ten tines more than what He received. Avasthi said that he did not know about that but he was penniless. Naturally, Jog lent him hundred rupees for the return journey. Jog further said, "If you say Baba has taken more than six hundred rupees from you, I assure you you'll get a promotion of fifty rupees per month." Avasthi accepted the loan from Jog and woefully told him that he had no god-father in the judiciary to get him a promotion. After the vacation ended he learnt he was given enhancement of fifty rupees per month.

In May 1913, Mr. Pradhan took a sum of three thousand and eight hundred rupees and overstayed his intended visit at Shirdi on account of Baba's insistence. Baba's unuttered and evident practice with those He loved was to deplete them of their resources. "I take away the wealth of those I love," Baba used to say. When he returned from Shirdi, his money was reduced to minus twelve hundred rupees. In fact, he had to borrow that sum from some one. In 1918, Baba asked Pradhan for a 'dakshina' of a hundred rupees. After receiving the amount he made certain signs which were not clear to him but they seemed to suggest, "Even if the heavens tumble down on you, do not fear, I am with you." After Baba's samadhi, Mr. Pradhan was appointed second class magistrate from 1926 to 1929. He was elected member of the Mumbai Legislative Council for two years. In 1927 he was made Rao Bahadur.

After H. V. Sathe retired from service there was some trouble about his pension. The pension department at first treated his last permament post and ignored the promotion he had got in between. So, he was a loser by fifty rupees per month. Sathe filed an appeal as he felt the order was totally unjust. When at Shirdi Sathe mentioned to Baba the injutice that had been done and said he would rather forgo the entire pension than accept the smaller amount granted to him. Baba in His own pungent slang assured Sathe He would force the fellows to do him justice. When Dhumal, the Nasik lawyer had gone to Shirdi, Baba depleted his resources. There came a time when he had no money but Baba wanted fifty rupees more as 'dakshina'. When he said he had no money Baba asked him to get it from Sathe. When Sathe was approached for fifty rupees for 'dakshina' he jumped with joy and gave him the amount he asked for. Sathe later succeded in the appeal which was heard and decided by Mr. Curtis. And Baba's direction to Dhumal to go to Sathe for the money, was just an indication of Sathe's forthcoming success. The order for payment of higher pension to H. V. Sathe was miraculously dated when Baba had demanded 'dakshina'.

In 1917, Gajanan Narwarkar was on his death bed. He sent five hundred rupees to Baba as 'dakshina'. He got cured immediately. This was a miracle for the doctors attending on him.

Balwant Hari Karnik says that Baba took from him a 'dakshina' of ten rupees at his first visit. That left him without money for the return journey. But just at that critical moment, a friend turned up and lent him the necessary money.

Another time, the couple wanted to go to Pandharpur and other holy places. On the way they halted at Shirdi. There Baba took away as 'dakshina' the entire amount they had because of which they had to give up the idea of a pilgrimage to other places. When Baba gave them permission to leave they didn't have the money even to go back home. Again the same friend came to their rescue. He lent them money. One effect of his contact with Baba was that he got premonition of the coming events and the courage to face them.

H. V. Sathe and Daji Lele were going to Shirdi to see Baba. On the way they got down at Kopergaon and there Lele happened to go to the library and got to see the gazzete. He discovered that he had been given an increment from Rs. 125 to Rs. 150. Then he came to Shirdi and bowed before Baba. At once Baba said, "Bring Me Rs. 25." The man said that he had no money. Baba retorted, "It is only yesterday I gave you Rs. 25. Go and bring the money." So he had to borrow money from H. V. Sathe. It was simply to show them that He was taking from them the fruits of what He had given them previously without their knowledge.

Mr. Clark says that he was very poor when he went to Shirdi Sai Baba. At first in 1913, he was earning only Rs. 100 per month. Baba would ask him for 'dakshina'. At times, He would take away all that he had in his pocket. Once he had just eight rupees. He took it away as 'dakshina'. After he said that he had no objection to parting with every pie, He stopped asking for 'dakshina'. He never came to harm by giving what he had.

'Dakshina' was used by Him to convince many of His devotees of His wonderful knowledge, by asking for the exact sums that were intended to be paid and prevented His men from lying.

Kashinath Garde, a sub judge, went to Baba who asked for 'dakshina' of two rupees and on the next four days, a rupee every day. Later, the next day when Garde had only three annas and six pice, Baba said to him, "Why keep those three annas and six pice left? Give them also to Me as My 'dakshina' and God will give you plenty. Don't worry." And Garde, without a word, gave away that amount at once.

Dattatrey Rasane, son of Damodar Anna Kesar of Ahmadnagar, was the fruit of Baba's benediction to Anna. Anna had no sons. Dattatrey went to Shirdi when he was twelve years old with an elder cousin. They had taken hundred rupees and Baba took from them ten rupees at one time, fifteen rupees at another time and in this way exhausted most of their stock of money until they had only twenty-five rupees. So they wrote at once to Ahmadnagar to obtain more funds so that they could give 'dakshina' to Baba and also for their return journey. That very evening Baba asked Dattatrey's cousin to give 'dakshina' of twenty-five rupees, the exact sum in his pocket. When they said they had no money to spare for 'dakshina' since the money they had was meant for their return journey Baba retorted, "Why talk all this humbug? You have got twenty-five rupees in a corner of your pocket. The money order will reach here tomorrow. Have no fear." And the cousin emptied his pocket without a word.

When once Baba asked for 'dakshina' from R. B. Purandhar he gave every thing from his pocket and thought he had nothing left; He felt elated for giving his all to his guru but Baba said to him, "You have still a two anna piece in your pocket, see." When Purandhar checked and he found a two anna coin he gave that coin also to Him.

Kolambe was under the impression that he was exempt from 'dakshina' because Baba was pleased with him as he had given up drinking and smoking. Still whatever money he had, he kept it with Sombre in case Baba asked him for 'dakshina'. He could truthfully say that he had no money. When he was in the Mosque, Sombre offered Baba 'dakshina' when Kolambe was also there. Baba also asked Kolambe for 'dakshina' of two rupees. Baba pointed towards Sombre and asked him to get it from him.

Most of the time Baba realized the sum that people really wanted to offer. Neither more nor less. Once, Mr. Pradhan planned to give twenty silver coins to Baba as 'dakshina' but when Baba asked him for 'dakshina' he offered Him a gold coin worth fifteen silver coins. Baba wanted silver coins instead of the gold coin. Mr. Pradhan had no problem. He gave fifteen silver coins the exact equivalent of the gold coin. Baba said that was ten rupees and not fifteen. So He wanted five more silver coins and the said amount was instantly handed over. In fact, Baba in the garb of wrong calculation, got the amount which .Mr. Pradhan had initially wanted to offer at Baba's feet.

G. K. Rege says that Baba asked him for 'dakshina' and he gave him five rupees. But He wanted five rupees more. Rege did not know why but he gave the demanded amount. Then, Baba remarked, "Nothing more is due to Me from you." He discovered the reason for demand only after he returned home. His wife told him that she had sent five rupees by money order to Baba a year ago and that money order had come back, with the endorsement that it would be realized in person. That is why Baba asked him in person for five rupees.

Rustamji Shahpuri Wadia of Nanded wanted to offer Rs. 5 to Baba. But Baba said that He had already received three rupees and fourteen annas. From him only one rupee and two annas were due. It was a mystery how and when Baba had received that amount. The mystery was solved when he went back and saw his accounts. A few days prior to his Shirdi visit he had entertained a Maulvi and He had spent that amount on him. It was to show him that He was one with other saints and gods. He made him realize that there is no difference between a Maulvi and Baba and so He did not want to receive a pice more than Mr. Rustamji wanted to offer.

In 1917 Hari Karnik of Dahanu on a visit to Shirdi had already obtained permission to leave when it occurred to him to offer one rupee more by way of 'dakshina'. When he tried to go back, another devotee informed him that as he had already been granted leave, he should not approach Baba again. So, he had to restrain himself. On his way back home he stopped at Kale Ram temple at Nasik. No sooner had he stepped inside, than the caretaker of the temple said, "Give me my rupee." Karnik paid the money willingly. This incident convinced him that Sai Baba had known about his last minute wish and this was His way of obtaining the rupee Karnik had wanted to give Him.

When Yashwant Galwankar went first to Shirdi, he started from his lodging but on the way to the Mosque, he recollected that Baba would ask for 'dakshina' from him. So, he went back and brought two rupees to offer Him. Then when he went to the Mosque, Baba asked him for 'dakshina' He paid Him two rupes and He did not ask him for more.

In 1909, when Dube was at Kopergaon, a lady from Aurangabad took a loan of ten rupees from him. At that time very casually she talked of a saint, Sai Baba of Shirdi. Dube had heard this name for the first time. He vowed that he would offer the amount to the Shirdi saint in case he got the loan amount back. But infact he was doubtful. By chance he went to Ahmadnagar and happened to meet that lady who returned the money! So he went to Shirdi to see the saint. On the very first day Baba took ten rupees from him. He was there for a couple of days more but Baba didn't ask him for even a single pice more.

Anand Badave says that in 1906, he went to Shirdi and as usual Baba asked him for 'dakshina'. When he paid some amount Baba wanted more. He repeated this several times till his funds were practically exhausted. He wanted to give another rupee but somehow failed to do so as by that time he had got permission to leave and so he could not go back to Baba. He returned and told his wife about it. Some years later he fell on bad days. His finances were low and he was running from pillar to post, getting little or nothing. Then his wife reminded him that he had wished to pay Re 1 to Sai Baba and had omitted to do so. At once he sent a rupee to Sai Baba by money order. Immediately, the tide turned for the better. He had very good days and no difficulties after that.

Dhumal had won a case very miraculously due to Baba's grace. He didn't have to take trouble for that case. Yet he got Rs. 300 for it. When he went to Shirdi, Baba took three hundred rupees from him as 'dakshina' in instalments. Dhumal knew he had no right over the money as he didn't have to make efforts to win the case.

Once in the presence of Shanta Ram Balwant Nachane, Baba asked Balkrishan Vaidya for sixteen rupees as 'dakshina'. Vaidya pleaded want of money. A little later, Baba asked for thirty-two rupees. Then He put forward the demand for sixty-four rupees. At this both Nachane and Vaidya told Baba that they were not rich enough to pay such huge sums. Then Baba asked them to collect the amount and then pay. This proved to be a prophecy. In the meanwhile Baba fell sick. A 'namsaptah' (non-stop chanting of God's name for full one week) was observed for Baba's health and it had to be followed by a grand feast to be given to all comers on a large scale. Money had to be collected. At Dabholkar's bidding Nachane and Vaidya started with an empty hat in their hands. The collection they totalled sixty-four rupees and it was sent to the people who were organizing the feast.

There were times when Baba flatly refused to accept any 'dakshina.' Once an immoral man who was leading an adulterous life came to Baba and unasked offered Him five hundred rupees as 'dakshina'. Baba burst out, "I want none of your money of sin. You are keeping a mistress. You take it back and give it to her." And the man quietly went away.

Even costly gifts were not accepted. A lady from the royal family of Baroda came for Baba's 'darshan' and brought two plates full of silver and gold coins. Baba didn't accept her gift. She wanted to give it to Mhalsapati. Baba didn't let him accept the gift either.

Sometimes 'dakshina' was collected to instil faith in the newcomer. Chakranarain, the income tax officer who had been sent to assess Baba's income, says that once a police officer went to Baba. Baba asked him for 'dakshina'. The officer replied that he had nothing. Baba then asked him to check his pocket as there was a fifty-rupee note in it. The note was then produced and offered to Baba but Baba wanted only a small amount as the officer would soon be in trouble and need the money. So indeed it happened. He had to use that balance to extricate himself.

Bibliography

	BOOKS	WRITERS
1.	Life Of Sai Baba Of Shirdi Vol. I	Sh. Narsimha Swami.
2.	Life Of Sai Baba Of Shirdi Vol. II	Sh. Narsimha Swami.
3.	Life Of Sai Baba Of Shirdi Vol. III	Sh. Narsimha Swami.
4.	Devotees' Experiences Of Sh. Sai Baba	Sh. Narsimha Swami.
5.	Shri Sai Satchrit	Sh. Govind Rao Dabholkar
6.	Shirdi Diary Of	Sh. G S Kharparde.
7.	Sh. Sai The Superman	Sh. Swami Sai Sharan Anand
8.	Sh. Sai Baba Of Shirdi	Sh. M W Pradhan.
9.	Sai Baba Of Shirdi	Perin S Barucha.
10.	Sai Baba The Master	Acharya E Bhardwaj.
11.	The Incredible Sai Baba	Arthur Osborne.
12.	Experiencing Sai Baba's Shirdi A Guide	Allison Williams.
13.	Sh. Sai Baba Of Shirdi A Unique Saint	M V Kamath And V B Kher.
14.	Eternal Sai Baba	S Maneey.
15.	Shirdi Sai Baba The Universal Master	Dr. S P Rohila.
16.	The God Who Walked On Earth	Rangaswami Parthsarthi.
17.	The Divine Glory Of Sh. Sai Baba	Chakor Ajgonkar
18.	Life History Of Shirdi Sai Baba	Ammula Sadashiv Rao.
19.	Hriday Ke Swami Sh. Sai	Vikas Mehta.
20.	Prithvi Par Avtaratit Bhagwan	Rangaswami Parthsarathi
21.	Shirdi Ke Sai Baba	Dr. Rakesh Shastri.
22.	Teri Haiyahi, Sab Ka Swami Sai	Amar Singh Gautam.
23.	Shirdi Sampuran Darshan	Dr. Rabinder Nath Kakarya.
24.	Sai Hari Katha	Dr. Rabinder Nath Kakarya.
25.	Shirdi Sai Baba The Saviour	Dr. Rabinder Nath Kakarya.
26.	Sh Sai Baba Ke Ananya Bhakt	Dr. Rabinder Nath Kakarya.

27. Sai Bhaktanubhav — Dr. Rabinder Nath Kakarya.
28. Muktidata Sh. Sai Baba — Dr. Rabinder Nath Kakarya
29. Sh. Sai Baba Ke Param Bhata — Dr. Rabinder Nath Kakarya.
30. Sri Swami Samarth Maharaj of Akkalkot — N S Karandikar
31. Shirdi Sai Baba and Other Perfect Masters — Cb Satpathy.
32. Shirdi Saibaba (An Epic) — Basavaraj Gunaki
33. Guru Charitra — P B Paranjape Alias Nana

Glossary

HINDI	ENGLISH
Avatar	incarnation
Anna	a coin used in India in the past, it was 1/16th part of a rupee.
Arati	waving of lights in front of a god, a Hindu way of worship.
Ashram	an orphanage, an abode of saints. A place of refuge
Abhishake tirath	water that has been used to bathe and idol/Baba.
Akshat	yellow rice meant for worshipping.
Brahmchari	celibate.
Badam	almonds.
Beta	son.
Bel	a variety of plant.
Bhindibhaji	a dish prepared with ladyfingers.
Brahmbhoj	a feast for the community.
Bhagat	a devotee, a disciple.
Bhajan	singing of religious songs in chorus.
Chawadi	a public meeting place of menfolk in a village.
Chillum	a clay pipe.
Chapati	a flat bread.
Dakshina	cash offerings to gods or saints.
Darbar	court of a king.
Darshan	sight or view.
Dhuni	sacred fire.
Faqir	a Muslim saint/ ascetic, a beggar.
Faqiri	sainthood / wife of a faqir.
Goshala	a place where unwanted, barren cows and old bulls are kept.
Gangajal	sacred water of the Ganges.
Guru	a guide, a teacher.
Gerua	orange coloured robe.
Greh pravesh	celebrations prior to entering a new house/ house warming.
Khichdi	a dish prepared with rice and pulses.

Kazi	a religious leader of the Muslims.
Kafani	a long gown used or worn by 'faqirs'.
Kakad arati	morning 'arati'.
Kirtankar	lead singer in a religious gathering.
Mala	a garland of flowers or beads.
Mahasamadhi	A yogi's conscious exit from the body
Mandir	temple.
Masjid	mosque.
Moolnakshatra	a constellation of stars, which is inauspicious for the father.
Navaidya	food / eatables offered to gods.
Prasad	navaidya when it is distributed among the devotees is called 'prasad'.
Pandit	priest.
Pooja	worship.
Pujari	a priest in a Hindu temple.
Prachar	propaganda..
Pista	pistachio.
Peta	head gear.
Pir	a Muslim saint.
Rudraksh	sacred beads – seeds, which grow on a tree.
Sadhu	saint, one who follows the path of 'sadhna' ie spiritual discipline
Sanyasi	a saint, one who has given up worldly things/monk.
Sehra	ornamental arrangement of flowers.
Sataka	a wooden rod.
Samadhi	mental equilibrium / final resting place of a dead saint.
Samadhi Mandir	a place where mortal remains of Sai Baba have been kept.
Satpurush	an elevated man.
Sevadar	servant.
Sahukar	money lender.
Shirdikar	a resident of Shirdi.
Shilajit	name of a tonic.
Saligram	a black stone for worshipping.
Sloka	verse in religious books.
Tonga	carriage driven by a horse.
Tongawala	a tonga driver
Til	sesame.

Glossary

Tamsik bhojan	non- vegetarian food.
Tulsi	a sacred plant .
Udhi	sacred ash.
Urs	annual festival in honour of a Muslim saint.
Wada	a house, a resting place.
Yoga	a combination of physical and spiritual exercises / scientific technique for God realization
Zari	embroidery with gold or silver thread.

Eleven Solemn Promises as Pledged by
Shirdi Sai Baba

For Material Success, Prosperity & Happiness

1. Whoever comes to my abode, their suffering will come to an end once and for all.

2. The helpless will experience plenty of joy, happiness and fulfilment as soon as they climb the steps of the Dwaraka Mayee.

3. I am ever vigilant to help and guide all those who come to me, who surrender to me and seek refuge in me.

4. There shall be no dearth of any kind in the houses of my devotees. I shall fulfil all their wishes.

5. If you look to me, I shall look to you and take care of all your needs.

6. If you seek my advice and help, it shall be given to you at once.

7. If you cast your burdens onto me, I shall surely take them on and relieve you of them.

8. I shall be ever active and vigorous even after casting away my body.

9. I shall respond and act in human form and continue to work for my devotees from my tomb.

10. My mortal remains will speak, execute and discharge all the needs of my devotees.

11. My tomb shall bless, speak and fulfil the innumerable needs of my devotees.

www.ingramcontent.com/pod-product-compliance
Lightning Source LLC
Chambersburg PA
CBHW071114160426
43196CB00013B/2562